THE EMBARRASSING-MEMORY MURDERER

The disaster that was my foolish year desperately trying to finally overcome being that weird, short, fat, shy, penisless, quiet loser you used to pick on in school

DAVID TIECK

Author of *Losing My Virginity 52 Times*

iUniverse, Inc.
Bloomington

THE EMBARRASSING MEMORY MURDERER

The disaster that was my foolish year desperately trying to finally overcome being that weird, short, fat, shy, penisless, quiet loser you used to pick on in school

iUniverse books may be ordered through booksellers or by contacting:

iUniverse
1663 Liberty Drive
Bloomington, IN 47403
www.iuniverse.com
1-800-Authors (1-800-288-4677)

Because of the dynamic nature of the Internet, any web addresses or links contained in this book may have changed since publication and may no longer be valid. The views expressed in this work are solely those of the author and do not necessarily reflect the views of the publisher, and the publisher hereby disclaims any responsibility for them.

Any people depicted in stock imagery provided by Thinkstock are models, and such images are being used for illustrative purposes only.

Certain stock imagery © Thinkstock.

ISBN: 978-1-4759-6340-3 (sc)
ISBN: 978-1-4759-6342-7 (e)
ISBN: 978-1-4759-6341-0 (dj)

Library of Congress Control Number: 2012921988

Printed in the United States of America

iUniverse rev. date: 12/26/2012

"The rate at which a person can mature is directly proportional to the embarrassment he can tolerate"

Douglas Engelbart

TRY HARD

'There is only one memory from my life that I have both cried thinking about and jerked off thinking about,' I said into the microphone. 'I am, of course, talking about how I got dumped *halfway* through losing my virginity.'

It was late 2009, and I had descended into the bowels of an old building in Greenwich Village in New York City to perform stand-up comedy for the very first time. After well over a decade of being quite likely the shyest human being alive, I was about to do perhaps the most daunting thing I could imagine.

CB's Comedy Club was surprisingly packed, the crowd mostly made up of fellow rookie comedians, and I had decided that for my first performance, instead of telling a bunch of made up jokes, why not just go all in and share a humiliating story I swore I would never tell another soul.

After nervously sitting through a plethora of performances by shaky-voiced rookies telling jokes to a room full of shaky-handed rookies waiting to take their turn—meaning that pretty much everyone was far too worried about their own upcoming set to be in a position to laugh at anything at all—suddenly my name was called.

My knees trembled as I made my way to the microphone, and I was worried that when I tried to talk nothing would come out. I considered fleeing, but instead screamed inside my brain. 'Just fucking do it!' and my mouth opened, and my embarrassing story began to flow out.

As the above opening line left my tongue, something truly amazing happened; laughter rose up from the audience. Not belly laughs, mostly snickering, but I had officially earned my first ever stand-up comedy laugh. I looked out over the audience and noticed that faces were now looking up from their notepads. The rookies' attentions had been grabbed, and it was up to me to deliver.

I paused for a moment, and then told the following story:

On this fateful day, I was two weeks shy of my twenty-first birthday, caked in so much acne I looked like a burn victim, finally going through an awkward growth spurt and only part way to losing the excessive chub that had plagued my teens, as shy and timid as any human has ever been before and the only way I could have been more of a virgin is if Jesus suddenly plopped out of my genitals. I'd only even had my first kiss earlier that same year, and at this stage the most intimate thing I had done involving a girl was probably listening to one peeing through a bathroom door, thinking, 'Wow, a girl's vagina is exposed on the other side of that wood.'

The girl, on the other hand, was an impossibly gorgeous teenage blond, with a smile so amazing a mere glimpse made the skin melt off my body, and she was well practiced in the celebrated art of allowing men to stick their dicks in her holes. We'd been dating for around two weeks, by which I mean I'd make horrifically awkward phone calls to her every couple of days, and she refused to tell her friends about the time we'd made out once, or be seen in public with me.

Then one day, out of the blue, *she* called *me.* It was a stinking hot summers day and she called to say that she had consumed a few alcoholic beverages, that her dad was out of town, and she was bored and wanted to know if I'd like to come over. 'Maybe she wants to have sex' I joked to myself 'ha ha, you crack me up Dave, as if you'll ever have sex', then I had a minor panic attack about the thought of trying to make conversation, having already used up all thirty seconds of my repertoire talking to her on the phone, however failing to think of an excuse to get out of it, I decided to go.

When I arrived I found her at the door in a bikini top and short skirt. She put on a movie of some description, but we began talking over it. At this point of my life I had picked up a hobby of trying to learn new words and pepper them into my conversation in a pathetic attempt to impress people. With pathetic the only tool in my toolbox, this was the tactic I used now, and so I uttered some word new to me, but probably not new to most people over the age of twelve, something like 'zenith', 'plethora' or 'obviouslytryingtoohardyoumoron' and then I proceeded to immediately give her a highly pretentious definition of my fancy word. This pissed her off immensely 'I don't need a fucking definition, do you talk to all your friends like that or do just want me to know that you think I am stupid?' She snapped at me, and I apologized profusely, and then decided to let her raise the next topic of conversation.

Perhaps because she wanted to prove her age and experience to me, or perhaps because it was her plan all along, she chose the topic of sex. And perhaps because she wanted to prove her age and experience to me, or perhaps because it was her plan all along she now gave me a far too detailed description of her sexual history to date.

I was shocked to discover that although she had participated in numerous sexual acts, she had yet to receive oral sex. Being a gentleman, and well because the only thing I could think to say in this moment were insults towards the assholes that had got to her before me, I assured her that if she'd allowed guys to have sex with her, and given them oral, and they hadn't even offered to reciprocate, then they were assholes. I went on to say that I would go down on her anytime, anywhere. She told me that I was sweet, then she accepted my offer, and I threw up in my mouth a little, and took off her bikini bottoms.

I approached this task, which was a first for me also, full of panic, and with the strategy of a man in his twenties who has seen it done a million times in porn, but with an inkling that in the non-porn version I may have to omit jamming my entire fist inside her, and instead try to be gentle. Somehow, this approach actually proved successful; she moaned a lot, and then pulled my face to hers and she spat at me, '*Bullshit* you've never done that before!' At that moment I swelled with, among other things, considerable pride. Also, having performed my oral duties, and having had them received so well, I knew that if I didn't to go for that 'penetration' maneuver I'd heard so much about now, then I would remain a virgin for life.

Shocking myself monumentally, I did in fact go for it; I believe I actually asked for permission, as sweetly as I could of course, 'may I, now, um please, um if you don't mind, you know, um, fuck you now'. Given an enthusiastic yes I grabbed at my football team adorned Velcro wallet, and pulled out an extremely old condom, purchased in a grimy convenience store bathroom, unwrapped it awkwardly and then I rolled it on.

I did actually know how to do this, as I had done it several times previously; girls practice kissing on their female friends (apparently, and don't let me watch) and I sat at home practicing putting on condoms before falling asleep crying at the fact that I'd eventually have to pull it off without it being inserted into anything other than the hole in a melon! (Actually, I never tried this. I did have a special teddy though).

I was about to have sex. 'OH MY GOD I'M ACTUALLY GOING TO DO THIS!!!' I was thinking, as the inevitable HUGE problem became clear. It was a stinking hot summer's day, and I'd refreshed my thirst many times in the preceding hours, and my bladder decided it might, at some point in the very near future, need to be emptied. While my testicles swelled with semen, my bladder was putting up a stiff argument as to which liquid would emerge from my penis first. I had a quick debate. Risk her changing her mind while I was in the bathroom, or risk urinating inside of her?

I shoved him right on in.

Two seconds later, I had pulled off something I wasn't sure if I was capable of; I did not cum within the first two seconds. Two minutes later, I had achieved my second goal; I had not cum within the first two minutes! I was doing it, I was doing sex, and I was doing it better than hordes of laughing girls had suggested most guys do on their first time. Holy shit! And yes I was watching a clock the whole time. Holy romantic.

Six minutes later and my joy was dissipating; now I really, really, no doubt about it, desperately needed to piss—like really *needed* to. After making the two-minute mark I promised myself I'd focus on just enjoying it, but I began to panic that I still hadn't had my orgasm, and I needed to wee, and one now seemed far more likely to happen than the other. I had numerous options:

- Fake an orgasm, even though I had never had a one near another human and wasn't sure if I could pull off an accurate portrayal even upon having a real orgasm
- Fake a cramp in my left testicle (always the crampiest of the two)
- Say 'oh my god is that your dad coming in' and sneak off to pee while she frantically checked the door and his parking spot
- Make her cum so hard that SHE would have to take a break (ha ha, you crack me up Dave)
- Claim the condom had broken and run to the bathroom to check only to come back and say 'false alarm, and now where were we, and why do you look white with fear like girls who have a teenage pregnancy scare look like?'
- Proclaim to be Jesus reincarnated and say 'sorry, Dad says it's bad for me and the human race to waste my seed'. Or the worst of them all:
- Tell the truth

Like a trooper, I kept going as long as I could, but in reality there was only one thing I could do. I had to raise the white flag. I just HAD to stop. Yes—I literally had to pull my penis out of a beautiful girl's vagina, the first that had ever allowed me inside it, and then

I whispered into her ear the sexiest combination of words in the English language: 'I'm just going to the toilet.'

I needed to pee as quickly as possible and get back to that beautiful naked girl fast, but here I faced more problems. My penis was pointing at the ceiling, and the toilet was down at my knees, and worse, it had one of those toilet seats you have to hold up with your hand. I hate these goddamn things! Whoever designed toilet seats like that deserves to sit on a seat covered in urine every time they ever go to the toilet, ever again, you bastard! I got about two drops of urine in the toilet; the rest of it covered everything else in the room.

I couldn't leave it like that. What if she came in here before I had a chance to come back and clean it up? What if she discovered that I had stopped mid sex to go and piss all over her bathroom wall? What kind of a perverted psycho would I look like then? So I used about two rolls of toilet paper to clean up every discernible droplet of urine I could locate. This took, understandably, a considerable amount of time.

Eventually I returned to her, with a second condom in hand, ready to resume where I had somewhat abruptly left off. Unfortunately, she had other ideas. I found her far less than prepared for a resumption of affections; in fact, she had gotten dressed, and she was sitting on the edge of the sofa looking mightily displeased, completely clothed, and certainly no longer naked.

'What's going on?' I asked forlornly.

I stood there naked, with a still-raging hard-on, having failed to even COMPLETE my first attempt at sexual intercourse, it was now, in this humiliating state, that she coldly said to me, 'I don't think this is working out—I think it would be better if we were just friends!'

I pleaded my case, but she would hear none of it. It was the end. I was being dumped. Dumped, while being rejected, still erect, HALFWAY through losing my virginity, just like it always happens in Disney movies.

Once we had finalized the niceties and resolved to be firm friends forever more, I eventually slunk away to my car, where I proceeded to burst into tears.

Not content with this slight, a couple of months later I managed to win her back, but only long enough to fall in love with her, for her to cheat on me, and then dump me—again—for another guy.

The attraction to my rival was understandable; he stole cars for a living, unequivocally raising him up in her estimation so highly she was compelled to choose him over me. I loathed her for what she had done to me. I would have done anything to make her feel the hurt and shame she had thrust upon me. But there was nothing I could do; you can't hurt people who don't have any feelings for you, and she loved this other asshole, and he probably didn't even need to urinate while they made love.

Then one day, I heard, he physically beat her. So despite his admirable bladder control, the guy turned out to be all kinds of scum. In the succeeding years, I have wished terribly awful things to befall him, but unfortunately I haven't heard any stories of a guy fitting his description who, while trying to climb over a barbed wire fence, accidentally got his testicles ripped open, leaving him trapped there, where he bled to death over an excruciating year and a half. But, you know, some stories aren't 'newsworthy'; so there's always hope.

The kicker, though, and really this is the part of the story that made me carry this pain around for years on end, was that she dumped me for taking a piss mid sex, and yet she didn't even dump his ass for beating her up! This was a memory that would weigh me down in all sorts of painful ways for many, many years.

Of course, in my stand-up act, I now realized that I had ended my story on a super downer, so I fumbled around with my bits and pieces of paper and pulled out an actual joke, to go out on a high note: 'When I pick my nose and have nowhere to wipe it, I put the booger right back in my nostril—I guess I'm just a neat freak.'

It was by no means a perfect comedy set, or even a particularly funny one, but my story, which was all horribly true, got at least some laughs throughout, especially when I became animated and physically acted out things like trying not to urinate on the poor girl's wall. And as the night wore on, several other comedians who were bombing spectacularly claimed that I was so good for a first timer that I must have been lying about never having performed before, which was about as big a compliment as I could imagine, even if delivered in a backhanded kinda way, you assholes, it's not my fault you can't achieve mediocre like me!

But mostly, I was proud of myself, I had done something awesome; I had taken one of the most embarrassing moments of my life, something I had literally never told another single soul in the world, and laid it out for a room full of strangers, and perhaps foolishly my new girlfriend of just two weeks, who was sitting in the audience, and I had used this humiliation to make people laugh. And by making people laugh it seemed to make it all better.

This was *good*.

'Wait, am I now happy I have lived though so many humiliating moments?' I thought 'Maybe I should share more of those uncomfortable stories? Of course I should!' I said to myself 'And awesomely I have shitloads of them'!

INTRODUCTION

When I was young, my family had a cat named Frosty. I loved Frosty enormously and growing up with him left me a life-long cat lover. Frosty was a cat that spent the night outdoors, and seemingly spent his evenings hunting, and running all around the neighborhood and, I hope, having the time of his life. Sometimes though, like most cats, he would want affection—something I was usually more than happy to provide, because Frosty was awesome, and because only a really evil person would have a problem showing such a loving creature as a kitty affection, as I am sure you would agree, right?

One evening after Frosty had been put out for the night, and as I was ready to go to bed, I noticed he was sitting at the glass sliding door adjacent to our family room. I could see he wanted some attention, but I was tired, and didn't feel like going out into the cold to give him some petting or hold him in my arms. 'I'll do it tomorrow,' I distinctly remember thinking to myself.

When I woke up the next morning, Frosty was still in the same spot. He had died overnight. Right there, in that spot, wanting some love. Knowing that I had considered giving him the affection that he needed and then had made a conscious decision not to, out of pure laziness, crushed me, made me hate myself, and is still the single biggest regret in my life. Also did you agree with me above? If not you probably feel pretty fucking guilty now, right?

Cut to January 2010, and now several years after finally overcoming a couple of lazy decades of crippling depression, and things are actually going really great for me. My career feels as though it is about to take off, I spend my days and nights laughing, making people laugh and doing the things that I love, I have friends I truly care about, I am feeling attractive and healthy, and I am confident and happy, full of direction and optimism, and mentally and emotionally sound like I have never been before, and I haven't even been dumped in favor of a complete scumbag who punches girls in years. It was pretty sweet. And when things aren't broke, why try to fix them, right?

That's why I decided that it was the perfect time to finally try to fix all the mortifying things that have happened to me throughout my life. I mean I have always been a dweller, and forever full of regret. I am the type of person who can be sitting reading a book, watching TV, or sitting in a crowded restaurant, when for no apparent reason whatsoever I will recall some negative memory from my past, and I'll find myself muttering under my breath like a crazy person something like, 'I can't believe when you were seventeen you made fake boobs out of a cut-up sofa cushion to put under your pillowcase and fondle, you freaking loser!' These disintegrations always end with me hurling insults at myself, followed by sentiments such as, 'Someone please cave my head in with a shovel,' or 'My God, stab me in the face, stab me in the face!' (The face has always been my favorite place to imagine a person being stabbed 'why do you always think about people being stabbed in the face you psycho' being another of my mutterings). Who wouldn't want to fix stuff like that, right?

For my entire life, I have gone through this procedure several times daily, with a whole myriad of memories and regrets, from my earliest childhood blunders to my most recent muddle-headed down right fucking stupidity. And it had occurred to me that while the story of how I lost my virginity had previously been one of the most frequent memories to cause me to break out in bouts of deep self-hatred and admonishment, ever since using it as fodder for laughs at that comedy club, it had not plagued me in that way at all.

I had told the story a few times since, enjoying the laughs I got, and somehow I was realizing that through telling it in an amusing way, enabling other people to share in the ridiculousness and humiliation, I had killed the embarrassment of the memory. I had taken ownership of the embarrassment and in doing so had murdered it.

In life, sometimes we make mistakes we can never take back. I can never go back and give Frosty a cuddle. Who knows what was going on in his head, who knows if he was heartbroken that his family was inside and warm while he was outside and cold? Who knows if a hug to let him know I still cared would have prolonged his life? He was old, and his time was coming, so there likely wasn't anything anyone could do for the guy. But I would like to be able to say he died knowing I'd done everything I could to let him know that he was loved, and I can't.

The straight out reality is that my memory is full of many, many humiliations, regrets and unfortunate truths of my existence, sometimes I think quite possibly more than any human being who has come before, and most of which I have kept entirely hidden from even my closest friends and family members, and I was sick of letting them hold me down.

The plan was simple; I would allow a horde of my most discomforting recollections each inspire an adventure or challenge of some sort or another, make as much fun of at all as possible, and therefore take possession and control of them. Once something bad had led to something good then hopefully they would no longer feel the need survive my list of things I wish had never happened. I would be able to consider these bad memories murdered, with the ultimate intention of leaving me regret free, and as such free to be the best me I am capable of being. What could possibly go wrong?

The following are the essays, stories, jokes, rants, sordid reflections and brain vomits I wrote whilst attempting to murder embarrassing memories, during this truly wonderful and meticulously well planned year. These are all full of hope, love, and wisdom and in no way suggest that spending a lot of time obsessing over bad memories will affect you in any negative ways, and they are told with such lyrically gleeful excellence that I didn't feel any need to use bad language or disparage anyone, and cynicism and sex barely even raise their heads! My hope is they make you laugh and with that I can *finally* kill them the way I did with my first attempt at sex story, or else I'll fucking hurt some shit head, or some shit. I may really regret sharing all these stories, but don't worry, it won't be my biggest regret, I'll always have Frosty the cat for that. Oh also, for the record, I have never denied a kitty affection ever again, and that's pretty adorable of me, at least you think so, right?

CAN YOU STAND SOMEWHERE DIFFERENT, PLEASE?

Here we go! What horrible embarrassment should I tell you first? Ok, so when I turned twenty-seven, I decided to start writing a journal. I bought a shiny red diary and decided upon a theme: My successful attempts to be more outgoing.

You see, for much of my life I have been, I suspect, the single shyest human alive. I didn't just not talk as much as I'd like to, or hang back too much, or fail to speak my mind when I wished to, I spent my entire life simply struggling to get words to even come out of my mouth—and the very thought of having to talk to anyone was just agonizing. Sometimes I'd put off asking a simple question for days. Sometimes I'd put off making a phone call for weeks. Everything from calls to friends to important work calls. Risking being fired was worth avoiding the simplest of phone conversations. Forgetting the reality that if I were fired I would have to make a lot more calls trying to find a new job.

Without fail, if I had to talk to pretty much anyone at all, including family members and friends I'd had for years, I would panic, I would be filled with doubt, and I would be simply terrified that I would yet again freeze up as soon as I opened my mouth, and would not be able to think of a single thing to say. Unsurprisingly, I didn't like this.

I had been through ups and downs over the years as a result of this curse, and at the time I bought the diary, I was smack bang right down at the bottom of shy hell again, and I hated it. It made me miserable. And being a master logician, I reasoned that there could be no better way to spur myself on to bigger and greater conversations, exchanges of ideas, and lively debate among my peers, than staying at home every night writing my thoughts on the matter in a journal like an eight-year-old girl. Basically, the strategy was this: I had to write in it every day, and therefore I had to have done something worthy of an entry every day. I had to prove so outstanding at coming out of my shell that I needed to congratulate myself in journal form. The journal included entries like this one:

'I asked the receptionist today to send a fax for me after only an hour of procrastinating over it.'

Yes, that's correct—this was an entry detailing a *successful* attempt to be more outgoing. Leaps and bounds in a single day. I was such a smooth operator that I could compel myself to ask a workmate, whom I had known a long, long time, to do a simple task for me after 'only' brewing over how scared I was to talk to her for an hour. It was clear at this point that I should be a motivational speaker! *How to do stuff only really painfully pathetically pussy-balled losers need more than an hour to do* – a seminar By Dave.

I should also point out that this was a sweet kind woman who wouldn't hurt a fly.

Girl talk
'I love my boyfriend, he is so sweet he wouldn't hurt a fly'
Later that week
'I hate my boyfriend, he is such a pussy, wouldn't even come over to kill a spider for me, why can't I find a real man?'

Truth is for this real man here, being too scared to talk to this woman with such a simple request, was so insane I should have been institutionalized immediately (I really should have been).

And yet, in my shyness-befuddled brain, the episode marked some measure of achievement.

Another entry in this big book of success chronicled an evening I had summoned the willpower to go out wearing a new shirt AND new pants, at the same time! The fact I did this late at night in a remote area and still felt insanely awkward made this no less of a success for me. I simply had zero confidence in myself. I was a pathetic, pathetic fool, and you don't simply *jump* from pathetic to awesome in a single step, it is a process of gradual lameness reduction. After about three weeks, I could not face the constant daily challenge of putting myself out there so recklessly and relentlessly, so I gave up.

Quitting the red journal perhaps marked the lowest point of my life. Not only was I convinced that my very existence, the fact I continued to breathe, was so mortifying that I found imposing myself upon others for even the briefest of moments was unbearable, but I'd recognized it, tried hard to change it, and failed.

There was not a single thing about me I liked, so I had two choices - change every single thing about me - or die.

It was honestly a very tough choice. Thankfully, eventually, I pulled off a miracle and genuinely changed pretty much every little thing about me

When you wake up in the morning *trying* to remember all of your most embarrassing moments, as I have now begun to do, it can, dare I say it, make you feel a little depressed, which seems counter-productive as a path to happiness. With all of these thoughts running through my brain, the red journal kept popping back into my head. It marked a massive, and ultimately wonderful, turning point in my life, yet the memory of it still makes me feel awful. So I figured, why not start out this murder spree here, by slicing this little red diary of mine open, and letting it bleed to death all over some lovely white carpet?

I needed to do something that was the complete *opposite* of hiding shyly, frantically and quietly away. Now two things that have helped me rebuild who I am are travel and performing. Travel allows me to be anonymous, to not be judged, or burdened by people's expectations of me based on who I *was*, and just be who I feel like being in the moment. Performing let's me be other people entirely, or an exaggerated version of me, and in some ways therefore the realest me I can be. After much procrastination on how to begin this journey, fortuitously an opportunity arose for me to combine both these loves, and what could be better than assassinating my red diary memory, than by stepping out in front of as many cameras, lights and people as possible, with crowds all around staring at me, on the *red carpet* of a major film premier at the Cannes Film Festival?

And so it was, that I resolved to go to Cannes and represent, in the flush of fame and glamour, all for the sake of my newfound endeavor to murder my mentally torturous, embarrassing memories. Through some contacts I had made in the comedy and acting scenes I presently live among in Los Angeles, I somehow found myself with all the credentials needed to head to Cannes, pitch a couple of projects, and walk some red carpets alongside the celebrities and movie moguls. The world is like a poor unfortunate allergic kid—sometimes you just don't see the nuttiness coming.

With some friends in tow, we flew to Paris, and caught seventeen different forms of trains, buses and taxis south, before climbing onto a quant little yacht that would be our temporary home in Cannes.

I was here to walk a red carpet like a movie star and it occurred to me that I wasn't a move star, and I needed some advice on how to do this properly from someone who was. So I decided to entice gorgeous French/ Turkish actress and television personality Melissa Papel to train me up. I'm a guy who used to be unable to talk to the receptionist at my work - this will be easy.

AND NOW HOW TO WOO A BEAUTIFUL ACTRESS by Dave:

First develop an addiction to diet soda, my personal favorite is Diet Dr Pepper, but you may choose your own. This takes many years and results in lots of mocking and promises from friends that you will regret drinking so much of it when you develop bowel cancer, but it's about commitment.

Now find the one bistro in all of France that sells Diet Soda in conveniently enormous full liter sizes, order one, and proclaim loudly how very excited you are about it. Your extravagantly sized drink will now attract the awe and admiration of the beautiful actress Melissa Papel, who will come up to you and ask to take your photo. Simple.

Well, this is what happened to me, stuff that stupid rabbit-out-of-a-hat crap; it's diet soda that attracts beautiful actresses THAT'S magic—they should give that shit a show in Vegas! 'Now exclusively at the Bellagio Casino see the best magician in the world – giant diet soda! Buy your tickets now, only twelve shows a week!'

Over the next forty-eight hours I was to randomly run into Miss Papel two more times—clearly this was fate. There was only one thing for it; I had to stalk her!

She had mentioned to me that she often frequented the beach pavilion dedicated to the Turkish Film Industry, so I headed on down that way, hid behind some shrubs, snuck up behind some people—you know, anything to seem inconspicuous. I don't want to shock you, but we were NOT soon locked in a loving embrace. Seriously, I know it's hard to believe, but this DIDN'T work, she was nowhere to be found. I was gutted. Fate kicked me in the balls again!

Upset, I stumbled onto the beach, where, as this was the French Riviera, surely I should have the opportunity to console myself with naked boobs on display. However, (and I am worried about your heart holding up with this second shock so quickly in succession) there were NO girls displaying their breasts for horny strangers to gaze at. It was like I'd entered some bizarro land.

So I did what I had to do; I stripped off my shirt to expose my pasty white pudgy torso and announced proudly, 'Are you enticed, girls'? Still nothing.

It was time for a change of tactics – 'what do beautiful celebrities like to do?' I asked myself, 'they love to be on camera, that's what!'

'What is one of the things I am doing here in Cannes?' I proclaimed to myself with glee 'filming some footage in the hope of turning my past virginity-losing lifestyle franchise into a travel TV show, hell yeah. If only there were some way to combine these two things. Hmmm, hmmm, hmmm—wait, I've got it! I could call up Steven Spielberg and ask him to do me a favor; he could offer Melissa the lead in his next movie and in return she would have to, like, talk to me again. Only problem, I didn't know Steven, and he didn't owe me a favor. So how about this? I could ask her to be on MY show!'

Wow, I really am a genius sometimes. I found the business card she had given me and texted her and ten minutes later she was on the boat we were staying on ready to grant me my first ever on-air interview on how to best enjoy being on the red carpet, and she was wonderful, and beautiful and delightful.

She gave me advice on how to perform, such as walking slowly and enjoying the experience, and not to wave like I was doing a clichéd impression of the Queen (as I had planned), and to perhaps to put a hand in my pocket so I would look cool, and calm, and like I belonged there. She also stood so close to me I could smell her, and she was yummy. And I was so at ease with her that I twice joked about the dog poo adjacent to where we stood.

The lesson is, seriously guys, don't stalk girls. Just tell them you have a TV show you want them to appear on and then talk to them about poo - it's way easier, and the show can even end up not existing, because it turns out those things are really hard to get produced! (My mini-pilot can be found on YouTube, if any of you are curious, or a multi-millionaire television producer). So no stalking, well, ok, so I once heard a story from an old married couple where the man said he would show up at church really early every Sunday so he could see where she sat and he could sit somewhere he could watch her, until he eventually talked to her after a year, and after asking her out twenty or thirty times she eventually said 'only to shut you up' and they have been married for over fifty years! He 'just had a feeling she was the one' he said, so if you're thinking of stalking someone, ask yourself: Do you have a 'feeling?' and also are you stalking her somewhere nice, like a church?'

Please note:
- A boner is not a 'feeling'.
- Her bedroom window is not a 'church'.

A couple of hours after Melissa left, I had combined a pair of black skinny jeans (a clothing product I promised I would never wear - I hate fashion followers, 'cause, you know, what did I say about not stalking? Well, following fashion is just as bad as following a person - it's all following people) and a tuxedo jacket, shirt and bowtie I bought for $40 in a thrift store, and turned them a makeshift tuxedo (an outfit I had never worn and didn't think I ever would) and pulled together my unfortunately ill, but ravishingly beautiful partner in crime and date for the evening, Faith. Dressed up and ready to dazzle with our red carpet tips and hand in pocket nonchalance, we climbed out of the awesome houseboat and made our way toward the festival.

As soon as we got near the Grand Théâtre Lumière, hundreds of photographers began to jump out at us from every corner and they couldn't keep their lenses off us. They seriously lavished us with attention in a complete frenzy. This would formerly have been one of the world's biggest nightmares for me, but instead I was beaming with joy—even after learning these people were actually just fake paparazzi who take photos of nobodies to make them feel like somebodies, and then try and sell you pictures. It didn't matter that I was asked numerous times to step aside so photographers could shoot Faith without me; I mean, she was wearing seriously what was and is the most beautiful dress I have ever seen, so I was able to detour my usual self-hating mind, which was telling me that 'it's because I don't look attractive enough to be photographed by them'. I didn't care. I was happy.

Abruptly, we were on the red carpet proper, where it was absolutely chaotic. It was not like the Academy Awards, where journalists are lined up, and publicists are organizing interviews left, right and center. The Grand Théâtre Lumière red carpet was short and wide. Photographers stood on ladders and chairs, creating an entire wall of flashing light on both sides. The carpet was filled with people from all aspects of the film industry, from all corners of the world, and everyone was desperately trying to get at everyone they could, just in case it turned out you were a huge star in Bulgaria and a picture of you could be sold to *Bulgarian Soap Opera Digest* for half a million Bulgesos.

As we stepped into the line of fire, we were assaulted by light. Faith, who has far more show business experience than me, was clearly overwhelmed with emotion and awe, and began to walk fast. I wanted to just stand still, raise my hands up in the air and yell, 'You never stop surprising me, do you God?' But I tried to remember my advice from Melissa, and perhaps found my hand in my pocket at some stage. I grabbed Faith's arm to slow her up, and so we could walk arm in arm (and I could look glamorous by association), but it was far too chaotic to even consider picking out people to wave to. So while trying to look as Bulgarian Soap Operaish as I could, I posed briefly for seven million cameras, took in as much as I could in this tiny amount of time, and we walked inside, smiles glowing all around. (Damn it, why didn't I buy some of that teeth-whitening toothpaste?)

Once inside, we found our seats in the monumental theater and settled in to watch a film so painfully bad that I can't even begin to bring myself to say its name here. Although, with nothing in the way of entertainment on the screen, I did have time to sit and ponder what I had now officially begun. From a red journal of pathetic shyness to walking the hell out of my first ever red carpet at a major movie premier at the Cannes Film Festival, this murder dealy was bound to send me into some deeply painful memories, but if it was going to inspire experiences like this, then it was going to be awesome. Plus, there were hot girls all around me, and who could complain about that?

MY SPLENDID TEMPTATIONS

By the time I reached my mid teens, I was still a long way from hitting puberty. I recommend late development! When your friends are already starting to have sex and you're still years away from growing a pube, life is a dreamy wonderland. You get to have all sorts of fun.

Despite missing out on all the life-enhancing aspects of puberty, I did still get to experience some of the horrible parts, like endless unwanted erections. But seeing as my penis wasn't also growing in non blood-engorging ways, I treated these in unusual ways.

For example, I'd occasionally choose to walk around encouraging its viewership rather than hiding it; you see, for a while I somehow fooled myself into thinking this small pointy bulge would make people think I had a large penis! And all the gasps, stares, and laughter I received seemed to confirm this for me.

'Hey ladies, check it out! I have a chapstick in my pants.'

When in a less exhibitionist mood, I would experiment with various methods of erection eradication. One method that worked for a while was pushing down on it hard so the pain would scare it off like a lion biting off a springbok's face. This became my default move for a while—until I got caught doing it really obviously in math class with *lots* of people looking on. Every now and again I think I forgot that *feeling* invisible doesn't mean you *are* invisible.

There I was, sitting in class, thinking I was being surreptitious, when algebra gave me a boner, and frustrated I suddenly gave my penis a fast, hard shove, a good foot from being hidden under the desk. Lots of boys saw. And I saw them see, and I saw them show me with serious smirks that they saw me see them see.

Now panic overwhelms my body. My defense mechanisms let out a huge laugh, to try and let them know that my 'joke' or 'trick' had 'fooled' them so it was they who deserved the ridicule not me, but I could not only not think of a way to explain what the 'joke' or 'trick' was, and instead I began to shake my head back and forth as if my body and soul just needed to silently scream 'NOOOOOOOOO'!

The boys too don't quite know how to react. So they start laughing awkwardly as well, as if telling me 'what you just did is the most humiliating thing anyone has ever done, and we just weren't prepared for an opportunity to mock you of such magnitude and our brains seriously can't deal with it yet'.

Now our weird laughter attracts the attention of our teacher, a pudgy man who wore shorts every day of the year regardless of the weather, and looked like he should be in the 1950s, and he is not happy 'what the hell are you boys all laughing at' he bellows. 'Oh no' I mumble, as I descend into an alter-universe headspace of fear and fantasy that I am not sure if I have ever left since.

The kids say 'it was David's fault' and are asked to elaborate. If they don't tell the truth they will get into trouble, and if they do explain what they saw - 'David just bizarrely violently attacked his tiny boy sized boner' then my life is officially over. These guys don't want to get in trouble, but they can't even begin to explain what I just did.

We are angrily instructed to get back to our work, and I instead have a mental breakdown with fear of just how bad my life will be once every kid in school is told of what I have done. All of the possibilities play out in my mind:

- I will hear this sentence a hundred times a day 'I'd be angry at my dick too, if it was as small as yours'
- I will get a new nickname 'Tiny Dick Dave', 'very small violent cock', or 'the bruised boner boy'

- I will get punched in the groin everyday with the defense '*you* hurt your penis, why can't I?
- I will be attacked and depanted in the school yard so the kids can see the truth
- I will have the event turned into a pantomime for all the boys to perform in front of me daily
- I will be accused of being some sort of warlock and murdered and hung to death in the playground

Incredibly it was never mentioned. This was almost worse. I was teased and bullied mercifully still, so it wasn't out of kindness or respect, so I was left to think that people were just talking about it behind my back, that or maybe the following took place:

'Alright guys, we need to talk about what happened in Math'

'I know, what the hell WAS that?'

'Well we know he has a small penis, but it's not *that* small right?'

'That's not the point, why was he hurting it?'

'Look, I know that's where his penis *should* be, but it must have been something else right'

'You're right, no one would do that to their own penis, especially in class for Christ's sake.'

'Do you think maybe he actually had a baby corn in his pants that for some reason he was angry at so decided to crush?'

'No, I mean why would he have a baby corn in his pants? Then again that's more logical than him doing what he did to his penis?'

'Maybe he had a spider in there he needed to kill?'

'Or maybe he is actually a cyborg and that's how he turns on his math brain?'

'But who would have cyborg technology that good and yet be stupid enough to make such an embarrassing design flaw?'

'It just makes no sense'

'I say we just assume it does make sense and try and put this out of our minds!'

'We could just never think or talk about it again?'

'Phew. Yes. I NEVER want to think about that again'
'What should we do instead of bullying him over it?'
'We could have sex with girls.'
'Oh yes, great idea let's!'
'I mean it's not like David is going to!'

Then they all laugh at me so hard they nearly choked to death, something they blamed on me, hence why I was randomly punched so often.

The point, obviously, is that I've been making an embarrassing fool of myself from a young age, often involving my penis, while watching assholes get the girls. Maybe this is why I have spent much of my life dreaming of being an industrial-sized pussy magnet star of rock?

I joined my first band when I was fourteen. We were called 'Shed'. Cool, right? We never once picked up an instrument between us, but we designed numerous awesome logos.

Band two was a couple of years later, called 'Poikilothermic', and you know that is cool, because that is the scientific name for 'cold blooded'! Hell rockin' fucking hardcore motherfuckers. I was designated drummer for this one and because of this I actually took some drumming lessons. We never had a rehearsal, but the lead singer of that band now plays George Harrison in a Beatles cover band, so yeah, things were looking good.

Band three was bound to be right around the corner and hell yeah awesome, and a mere twelve or so years later that dream came true. 'Never Know' was incredibly good; we recorded around forty demos, wrote some genuinely awesome songs, and I was convinced, if I could learn to sing, that we were going to be the next Pink Floyd. Then my guitarist, Greenie, fell in love and suddenly the life of rock n' roll didn't hold the same appeal, and seeing as we were a two-piece band that left me kind of on my own.

Now, some of you may have just missed what I just said then, but I know some of you are screaming at your books going, 'What the fuck did he just say?' Because, yes, I said something totally fucking insane! Like certifiably, get him into Scientology to make him more normal, insane. I said, 'the life of rock n' roll didn't hold the same appeal.' I know! How is that possible?

When life was invented, someone asked, 'How is this going to work?'

'Well, it takes a man and a woman to make a baby, maybe we should base life around getting those things together and keeping them in one place of residence, we could call them something like a house and a family,' the reply came.

'That sounds ok, so we join a man with a woman, and then they'll just like work, and make more humans, and go to bed early. Ok, done—life is worked out.'

And meanwhile some other bad ass dude was off on a tour bus roaming the world, fucking seven girls a day, getting away with any shit he could come up with, being praised for his ability to consume mind-altering chemicals, and going on stages being worshiped for the art he made. And when he heard what these other people decided life was, he didn't really listen because his penis was currently in a nineteen-year-old girl's bum hole while her friend watched masturbating.

Is that the life I want? Yes, motherfucker, it is. (How many 'motherfuckers' is that so far? Maybe I'll tone it back a little for the easily offended motherfuckers. No, wait—rock n roll, motherfuckers!)

Cannes was over and my friends and I had headed to Amsterdam, to you know, have the kind of fun you can only have in a town sometimes re-named Amsterdamage. With killing off my bad memories like my lovely math class penis party on my mind I figured this was the perfect place to replace that memory with a bit of hardcore sex, drugs and rock n' roll.

A tulip is a bulbous plant in the genus *Tulipa*, comprising 109 species with showy flowers, in the family Liliaceae. - Wikipedia

Ok, what just happened? Why did I just talk about flowers? I'll tell you why, because when we got to Amsterdam we went and looked at the tulip markets. Yes flowers, those little colorful things which have smell or some dealy. For the record, two days later we were walking past a rose bush and my friend Faith smelled it and was like, 'Wow, this rose is like the most scented rose I have ever smelled' and then our other friend Bec smelled it and she was like, 'Wow, that's amazing' and so I was thinking, 'Hey this might be a chance to lose my virginity and smell a rose for the first time.' And so I do, and you know what? Nothing. I couldn't smell a thing. I didn't have a cold or a blocked nose, I could smell other things, but a rose by any other name still smelled like a cotton ball to me. I have tried again since, I can't smell flowers. It's true. Yet still, I'm in Amsterdam checking out flowers? Travelling with women sure is different from travelling with a pack of horny boys (Like a band? Yes, where is my band again?).

I had to cleanse myself of this monstrosity. At one point, a man in a flower shop got super pissed off at us for filming in his shop. 'Sorry, sorry, sorry, sorry, no film, no film, no film, no film,' he kept saying, but the truth is I think what he was trying to say in his poor English was, 'Seriously, dude, hookers in windows and you're looking at fucking flowers?' with a hint of, 'I live in the hookers-in-windows city and I sell *flowers*. WHAT KIND OF A MAN AM I?'

Sure we also looked at some awesome art, and Amsterdam is a city so beautiful it's a shame they didn't legalize drugs and prostitutes somewhere else and leave the 'dam to be free, and I did catch a glimpse of a couple of poor girls in windows selling their bodies for a living. But I went to Amsterdam and I didn't have sex, I didn't do drugs, and I did not fucking rock n' roll, but I *did* go tulip shopping!

I am supposed to be murdering embarrassing memories, not creating new ones.

And also, isn't perfume really just bottled flower farts?

There was only one thing for it—I had to pray. Having left Amsterdam we returned to Paris for a couple of last days of sightseeing before flying home. While there I went to Sacré-Cœur, the stunning cathedral on a hill in the Montmartre region of Paris, former playground for great writers and artists like Hemingway and Dali, Picasso and Monet, and here I lit a candle in a church for the first time (which seemed to bleed red blood for some reason when I lit it, unlike any other of the hundreds of candles lit by prayers—does that make me Jesus? Possibly, but more on this later). And I said a prayer for my career, asking god to help me inspire people, and entertain people, and asking for him to help my friends too, because I figure that God is nicer if you don't seem selfish even though he can read your mind doing it for selfish reasons and takes it out on you with bacne. This church thing wasn't doing it for me; God was the wrong god to pray to after my failures in Amsterdam. I had to go see a Lizard King

Sadly, Jim Morrison passed away very young while in Paris in exile from the United States after allegedly showing his penis on stage. Yes, Jim and I have something massive in common; we have both let our penises embarrass us and make our lives harder at times we weren't even attempting to use it for any of its intended purposes. And while choking on your own bloody vomit after too much alcohol and heroin is not a cool way to die, Jim probably doesn't care because when he lived he really fucking lived.

Faith, Bec and I went to the Père Lachaise Cemetery, a graveyard full of great writers, artists, and all sorts of great people from French history. I was able to press my lips up against the lipstick-covered Oscar Wilde grave (if I get herpes you're fucking dead, Wilde) and we walked the beautiful grounds, but we were there to see Jim, and that's why we couldn't find Jim anywhere for hours, until people started getting pissed off, and I had to leave them to somehow be pissed off even though they were in Paris, but it turned out it was for a reason. As soon as I was on my own, Jim grabbed my spirit and I was drawn straight to him, and within minutes right in front of me was a miraculous man's grave.

I was thinking I would get all rocked up and excited to see the grave of this wonderful talent, but I didn't; it was too somber a place. I was there to pray to Jim, and so I did.

Dear Jim,

I come to you today because I need guidance. Something really bad has just happened to me that I know you can help me with. I was in Amsterdam for a couple of days recently, and um, I didn't have sex, I didn't do any drugs, I didn't rock n' roll at all, instead, um (breaking into tears now), I went *tulip* shopping. And I know that's really going to offend you, 'cause it offended me, and I need you to help me bring back my artistic core and be a rock n' roller. So please, Jim (really losing it now), if God's standing in your way, just push him down (I was crying ok – DON'T JUDGE ME. Actually, I was acting that I was crying, because I had found my friends and got them to film this, but I will admit, as I let myself delve into a fake cry, a real one kind of burst into my heart), he'll forgive you, he's meant to do that, that's his job. I know you'll help me, Jim. Thank you. Amen. Light my fire (always reference the most famous song so he can't tell if you're a real fan or not).

It was the first time I had ever prayed to a dead rock star's grave. I am not sure if he heard me, or if God will give me even more bacne for telling Jim to push him over, but you know, when you do things like this, what really happens is you remind yourself what you want to do, and if I want to be more rock n' roll, then maybe I just have to do it on my own.

That's why Faith and I went and hung out at a cool café in Paris, and we sat and drank Champagne, and ate cheese and got all Frenchy, and I did some sketching and I wrote some poetry, and I reminded myself that the rock spirit lives inside of me, and the time is now to unleash this motherfucking beast onto the world!

By the way, I like to imagine what the corpses on either side of a celebrity grave think about having a celebrity neighbor:

Dead person to the right – Oh here comes more people, more people to trample all over me just to see Mr. Rock Star!

Dead person on the left – Speak for yourself, I'm just glad someone comes anywhere near me, I've been dead for over a hundred years, haven't had a visitor in fifty.

Right – See, the problem is your attitude, maybe if you weren't so needy people would come see you?

Left – Oh yeah, I'm the one with the attitude. You know what? I hope the next guy pisses on your grave!

Right – Well, screw you, maybe they'll be here for me, but I guess you wouldn't know what that is like would you?

Left – Fuck you, Kevin!

Right – No, fuck you... name no longer legible because your tombstone has been so poorly maintained!

Left – I'm going to KILL YOU!!!!!!!!!!!!!!

Right – No, I'm going to Kill YOOUUUUUUUU!!!!!

Jim Morrison –. You're both already dead, you morons, but if you'd like me to read you a poem, I can. Oh wait, sorry here come some more fans.

Right and Left - AAAGGHHHHHH

AND NOW SOME SURPRISING THINGS YOU MAY NOT KNOW ABOUT AMSTERDAM, By Dave:

- It has the most art galleries per-capita of anywhere on earth.
- Many of the buildings are sinking and look like they are about to fall over.
- If you go there and don't do drugs or have sex with a prostitute the day you arrive home the mayor of Amsterdam prank calls you pretending to be an aardvark.
- While marijuana is legal, to balance it out, watching squirrels play is strictly forbidden and I mean STRICTLY forbidden
- Before finding success with the red light sex district, Amsterdam previously failed miserably with the mustard-yellow painted chimney district.
- Seriously, you do not want to know what happens if you watch squirrels play, just trust me. If I talk about it anymore they might do 'it' to me too.

- The 'dam' in Amsterdam' has nothing to do with the dykes and everything to do with the premonition that Dave 'Dam' Tieck would, you know, visit one day.
- Trying to give yourself nicknames is awesome!
- Oh come on man, I can tell you're thinking about watching squirrels play, are you insane?
- You could have sex here with anything, even with a little baby corn in some kids pants that you're smashing because you're angry at it for some reason, that's why there are all those tulip markets, they're just fronts for baby corn stores.

MY BLOOD IS BETTER THAN YOURS

Birthdays were always a particularly happy time for me. The very day I was born a bridge collapsed in Granville, Sydney, allowing a train to fall onto a road, killing over eighty people and seriously injuring hundreds more. As I was being born, the hospitals all around Sydney were in frantic chaos. And of course on that day, as I am sure you remember, there were also the horrific Egyptian Bread Riots. Since then, other things that have taken place within twenty-four hours of my birthday have included a number terrible bushfires, the start of the first Gulf War and the devastating 1994 Los Angeles earthquake. Basically, if you ever turn on the TV and see blood, death, carnage, misery and signs the world is going to end, it's a good time to wonder if you've remembered to buy me a card.

As you can imagine, as a child I always looked forward to my birthday long in advance. I remember one special birthday when I told all my friends we were going to the mini-golf course for a wonderful day of playing golf in its most miniature form. The only thing I didn't understand was that when other kids had fun birthdays like this they had also mentioned this to their parents at some point. I really just thought the way these things happened was to just think they were going to. So all the kids showed up at my house, my dad said 'what do you mean "when are we going miniature golfing?"' followed by what for him must have been a bizarre argument before I spent the day crying from embarrassment and lack of miniature golf in my life.

A few years later I was having a skateboard-themed birthday and while transferring from riding over grass back to concrete, my back foot fell off the board and my front foot stayed on, resulting in my right knee scraping across the concrete just long enough to open up a horrific bloody birthday wound.

After a couple of hours the pain and grossness had even left me *blind*!

'I can't see, I can't see!' I was wailing

'Well, open your eyes,' someone replied, getting a huge laugh. Apparently my eyes were closed, that's why I couldn't see, blindness is a tricky idea for a 12 year old, but at least it's nice being a laughing stock on your own birthday.

The next day the wound had started to scab, and it was right on the spot on the knee where if I tried to bend my leg, the wound would re-open, and I was so horrified by the thought of more blood that I literally didn't bend my leg for a couple of months, even way past the time the wound had healed, and surviving several doctors appointments one of which included an injury absent x-ray.

My point being: I am actually capable of being really determined (except often when it would directly *benefit* my life) and I am not a fan of blood. I mean, it's really red and that's an icky color. Plus, you know, it comes out of rips and cuts in human flesh, which also is something I consider icky.

It was my penultimate night in Paris, and not wanting the trip to end I was having a late-night beer in a café, people watching and wishing some of them would happen to be girls wanting to show me a part of their body they bleed from monthly (seriously, Dave, a period reference while trying to talk about your pathetic attempts to get laid? Yes, David, if as divided sexes we cannot be open and forthright about our physical differences, how can we ever hope for equality? But, but gross, Dave. Equality, David, equality, we must have equality!) And well, to be completely honest, I had been complaining to friends recently that it had been so long since I had had any female attention that I would welcome just about any sexual interest whatsoever, just for the confidence boost.

Bad wish. Very, very, bad wish.

Since putting that out into the universe, I had been hit on by several gay men, and then by a woman in her forties who told my friend that she was looking for a man to 'sperm snatch' from.

Things could be worse. And I don't mean that in the clichéd comfort way: 'So what if you got fired and your wife is sleeping with your brother? It could be worse, have you heard of Africa?' which does nothing at all to cheer people up. In my case I mean things *proved* to get worse.

'Do you want to die?' a sixty-somethingish man with slicked-back grey hair, long fingernails and pronounced fang-like teeth said to me after suddenly sitting down opposite me and grabbing both my hands.

'Not really, feeling a bit young for that,' I replied.

'Cause I can show you another option,' he continued.

'Ok, so I am being hit on by a man, an old man, who thinks he is a vampire,' is what I should have thought before deciding it was bedtime.

Instead, I completely missed all these signs, as he had a way of looking into my eyes like a Jedi mind trick (Read: I was too drunk to really notice what was going on, same problem I assume those imperial storm troopers had—they had freaking awesome moonshine in galaxies far far away, why do you think people merely continue to drink in a bar after a man's arm has been sliced off?) and I let him spend some time with me while he tried to lure me away to a 'secret bar', in an underground spot, where they had '1000 different beers'.

So, ok, that's not so sinister. It was when he told me that he could help me live forever that I freaked out (or should have, but I was drunk, and he was speaking in metaphors, with broken French-accented English). And I was in Paris and in a good mood looking to have a good time, so I ignored this stuff. I even let him buy me a drink. I even bought him a drink back. I even kept chatting to him after the waitress tried to take away his not quite empty former beers and he responded by snarling and growling at her like a rabid dog.

I even let him suggest I order a special cocktail called an *Aphrodisiac* and when it came it turned out to be a warm beverage, which came in a wine glass, and looked like red wine, only with a slightly richer color and a familiar yet weird taste.

Yes, yes, I did all that. The drink was gross and I still finished it. (Yes, drunk, I know—I got to cut back on that stuff—more on this later). It was only after I had been 'rescued' by a local who had lived in Ireland for a few years, and I guess therefore had seen the bad things alcohol can make a young lad do, and then he and my friend Bec who was there started talking about the vampire who had been hitting on me, and that's when I realized I had just been hit on my a bloody vampire (ha ha, pun!), and had allowed myself at his bequest to drink a blood like beverage! By the way, Bec was convinced from the beginning he was a vampire, but didn't speak up till after I drank the blood. Hey, Rebecca, next time it's ok to tell me earlier, please! I was going to say I don't want to die, but I mean I don't want to live forever!

This is all true. What the hell is wrong with me?

So maybe it's ok to speak your mind once in a while, you know, to stop your friend from unwittingly becoming a vampire.

Of course, the lesson is twofold:

1. Start trying to murder your embarrassing memories and you attract vampires; and
2. Hey teenage girls, forget these *Twilight* vampires, come hang with me, I am the real life (sixpackless but occasionally not pale) deal!

Oh also, as a vampire, does that mean I can live forever by orally pleasuring women during their very special time of the mo… (Ok Dave, equality shmequality, now you're just being disgusting).

I guess the real test would be what happened next time I bled. By chance, the next time I bled was when I scraped my leg up against a loose nail while leaving a Mexican restaurant at Venice

Beach California a few weeks later and I opened up a surprisingly unrelenting gash. I was trying to mop up the blood when we went into a new-age type shop and when I smelled the incense suddenly something struck me like a poltergeist and a minute or two later I was lying on the ground on a dirty street feeling overcome with intense nausea and feeling like I was about to pass out, and that I was blind because I couldn't bare to open my eyes. It was powerful and scary and utterly wussy, I've bled so much worse so many other times, yet this time I felt like I was dying.

So there you go - proof my blood is now way more powerful than it once was, just losing a little bit of it makes me nearly DIE! Wow, imagine what would happen if *you* got some of my blood.

Speaking of death:

Never go to a PETA protest and throw a bucket of blood in a stranger's face before yelling, 'THAT'S THE FILTHY AIDS BLOOD YOU CURSED ME WITH! Oh wait, sorry, wrong person.'

Also,

Never go to a daycare and throw a bucket of blood in a toddler's face before yelling, 'THAT'S THE FILTHY AIDS BLOOD YOU CURSED ME WITH! Oh wait, sorry, I don't think that's even possible!'

Also,

Don't take drinks from strangers, unless you want a really awesome excuse to make really *wrong* jokes. Or else just blame them on the carnage in the world you were born into.

HEY, FELLOW HUMANS, YOU HAVE A REALLY SEXY EPIPHANY

Vampires, from what I can tell, aren't that picky. In the movie *Interview with a Vampire*, for example, Tom Cruise's vampire, when picking a mate, chose the decidedly average-looking Brad Pitt! Have some standards, you idiot.

Also, people always used to tell me 'you are what you eat', and I kind of wanted to be Brad Pitt for a while, all that most beautiful man alive kind of stuff, and so I figured I'd cut him up into bits and eat him. And get this, I did NOT become him! That whole 'you are what you eat' stuff is crap! Also, when I pooed him out, he was completely back to his normal beautiful self, that bastard.

Unlike those vampires, I am a superficial male. Most of my life I have been accused of being 'too picky'. 'Dave, you're way too picky,' my friends would say as a way of letting me know how they felt about my pickiness. In my defense, however, most of my life I always thought I'd be really lucky if a one girl ever loved me, and if it's only ever going to be one, she may as well at least be cute. That's not too picky, that's just a perfectly normal way of justifying your intelligent decision-making.

Having said that, I have *always* been too picky.

Part of this is just a defense mechanism. If I find something I don't like about a girl from a distance then I don't have to get the guts to talk to her, because *I* have already rejected *her*. So by finding ways to think beautiful girls ugly I got to be more of a shy loser, and everyone wins, especially the girls.

Then there was the time that for a while a few years back I had a bit of a flirty friendship with a girl who gave me clues that if I made a move she'd reciprocate and I held back because I wasn't sure if I found her attractive enough. She proceeded to go and win third place in the Miss Nude Australia pageant. *Only* the *third* most attractive nude girl in Australia, that's validation, right?

Of course, then I did end up later on sending her drunken text messages begging for sex, so I didn't turn her down completely.

Realistically, though, I do tend to have different taste from your average horny man. I prefer short girls with small boobs to tall girls with big, I like weird and big noses, I like quirky features, and I prefer no make-up and sneakers to glamour. So sometimes I will see a hot busty blonde in a hot dress, with a rich tan, perfect make-up and sexy heels and will out loud say, 'Eh, nothing special.' It's not that I don't find this attractive, I do—I find many, many types of girls attractive, but I am often simply more likely to find your nerdy friend's weird sister my kind of cute, especially if I know we have something in common, like severe mental issues.

To be perfectly honest, I spent much of my life not liking who I was. (The spellcheck dealy wants me to make it not 'who' I was, but 'that' I was—stop trying to make me suicidal Microsoft word, that's a whole different chapter of this book!) When you are so inclined towards such negative thoughts, you often find yourself wishing you were someone else.

Really, what I wanted was just to be a different me. Eventually, I found that different me and I am the completely well-adjusted normal boy writing these words right now. For example, here is a thought I had just moments ago:

I've decided to invent a sex act inspired by the ladle, because the ladle is the world's messiest serving device. Mmm, serving devices, sexy.

Now, clearly only a perfect stock-standard average-Joe normal person would think such things as a usual part of his day. Still, although I am way closer to the person I would like to be, there is the odd thing I would like to change about myself. I would like to be less picky, or more than that, acquire a more gracious way of looking at the opposite sex.

So I was in LA, having got back from Paris a day earlier, and was feeling bored and uninspired. I decided to go for a walk and try and find some fun. As I was walking past a movie theatre, I decided on a whim to go in and just see whatever was starting next, and lucked into Banksy's fantastic *Exit through the Gift Shop* about the street art scene and was now feeling entertained and mightily inspired.

As the opening credits rolled, I was thinking about the girl I had seen moments before entering the cinema waiting in line for tickets, and again at the concession stand. She was beautiful, impossibly so, wearing an oh-so-short skirt and a loose top showing off small yet perky breasts, and a cute face that she actually pointed at me and contorted into a small smile when I smiled at her while buying a Diet Coke. So, after the film, I decided to have a noodle around the posters for upcoming films and the small gift shop in the lobby in the hope to see her coming out of her own movie-watching experience.

As I flicked through coffee table books I looked up, hoping to see her and instead spotted another girl. My initial reaction was to think 'she's cute' before I immediately deconstructed her, moving past the initial cute face and noting things that I didn't like anywhere near as much. I thought back to the beauty I had encountered earlier and compared them, and then I felt bad for myself for never having experienced that beauty physically, but then also bad for judging these two girls like this without knowing stuff-all about them. After all, the girl I had noticed earlier was seeing *Sex in the City 2* and so quite possible had a horrible personality, whereas this new girl had a kind of bohemian look about her, suggesting that, to me at least, we'd probably get on really well.

I realized something about myself in this moment:

- I am back in a stage of really worrying about the wrong things
- I am still a superficial judgmental penis holed vagina face
- I hate the way I assume girls are always deconstructing me, yet I do it worse to them
- I actually let the 'how would people judge me if they saw that I'd I hooked up with *her*' enter my brain as I stare at something I initially found beautiful.

And most importantly:

- I am strangely allowing myself to look past beauty to concentrate on things adjacent to beauty and not beautiful, and
- I am a stupid tool asshole who needs to enjoy beauty whenever and wherever it is, because to do otherwise would be totally retarded

I made a decision right there and then to start looking for beauty wherever I could find it, and allowing myself to enjoy it without fearing judgment.

It was a wake-up moment, it was an epiphany, and in the moment it felt life changing. Or at least gave me an excuse to ogle more girls and feel profound.

Cut to ten minutes later. I was in a drug store picking up some painkillers for an injured friend (see, I am still a good guy, even if a judgmental one, who goes to the movies before delivering painkillers) and as I was waiting to pay I saw a staff member walk to the checkout and I immediately noticed her cool funky red dyed hair. Then I ran my usual list of faults and ruled her out as a potential mate. 'You judgmental wanker!'

However, now she served me and on the spur of the moment I did something out of character for me.

'I love the hair,' I found myself saying, not to flirt, but just to state a fact.

'THANK YOU!' she responded with an enthusiasm I am not used to receiving after complimenting a stranger randomly.

I began to think. You see, the thing is, in Australia we are taught to be modest and downplay compliments. 'Nice smile' gets 'Yeah, you know, I try to brush daily.' We don't accept it; we push it slightly to the side. Also, in life we learn to be wary of compliments, because we wonder about the hidden agenda. And thirdly, as a male often playing the 'wish I could get laid occasionally women-chasing game', we learn to be treated as such, and be caught out as not sincerely complimentary but rather as dirty wanna-be players saying anything and everything whether true or not, just for the chase, and we learn to receive disdain rather than thanks for complimenting a girl.

How have we allowed compliments to not be good? They *are* good. I want to give them, and receive them, and have both occurrences be happy. I made a commitment right there and then to spend the rest of this week randomly complimenting people as much as possible. Who knows how this will go, but, to compliment myself, 'it sure is nice of me to do it'.

Here are some of the notes I made over the next few days:

- Day two and I'm really struggling to send out compliments. Something in my mind keeps telling me that people don't want to hear compliments from someone like me. I love optimism.
- The same thing keeps coming up, the first thing I can think of to compliment is just something that stands out, and is usually something I actually feel the opposite of complimentary towards, like distracting earrings, too much make-up, or over-tanned faces. Is that why girls keep hanging onto these silly notions of beauty, because people compliment things that aren't actually flattering just because they are the easiest things to compliment?
- I want to randomly say to people, 'You're beautiful', but I just know that's now allowed. Why?
- I complimented the salesgirl at the cookie store on the bow in her hair with 'I like the bow.' She gave me a

'please don't hit on me' stare and intoned a withdrawn 'thank you'.

On night three I went out on a complimenting mission. I decided to go to *Happy Endings* on Sunset Blvd, because let's face it, I was complimenting *girls* (Compliment girls—best case scenario get laid or a date, worst case scenario they tell you to fuck off. Compliment a guy—best case scenario they tell you to fuck off, worst case scenario you get laid) so I figured where better to go than a college-aged kids' hangout equipped with beer pong, drink specials on a prize wheel, and well lots of beautiful young girls.

Frankly, it was tough going. Simply going up to someone and complimenting them is way harder than it should be. There was a group of girls that were wearing sports shirts with their nicknames on the back, and I complimented a couple of names and got told to go away. I called a girl beautiful and she replied 'fuck off'. I complimented smiles, outfits, hair, 'natural beauty' and I even complimented a girl's heels, and I HATE heels, all with barely a forced smile in reply. It was spirit crushing.

With my confidence struggling, and my shy and weak efforts to compliment girls for mostly things I didn't even want to compliment them on not going down too well, I did what any good complimenter would do, I got drunk off my ass.

Then I went on a complimenting bend so fierce it nearly ripped a hole in the space-time continuum's anus, and I got ignored like I was literally not even there, numerous times I got told to fuck off, and I stumbled around like a drunken loser until I just couldn't bare it anymore.

It was then something occurred to me – these LA girls don't god damn even deserve the compliments. So I wrote something totally illegible in my notebook (the only word I can make out is 'camel'), got pissed off and left.

New pact – compliment people who deserve compliments, this should be easier.

I headed to my local favorite diner, and it turned out a waitress I had a crush on there was drinking at the bar and I ended up spending the night lavishing her with compliments while she unleashed her hatred for the boyfriend she just broke up with for having a bad heart.

'He's an asshole'

'How could anyone treat someone as beautiful as you like that?'

'He never treated me nice'

'You mean he never told you how cute you are, and how cool your laugh is?'

She failed to notice the guy sitting next to her (me) with a heart so good I can't help getting it broken far too often, so I went into the night, drunk texting my ex asking her, 'Why am I un-lovable?' and fell asleep hugging the glass I drank one last cocktail out of. Compliments sure do make people feel good, but alas I had to let the experiment come to an end.

I should say this to you, my readers, I think you're all awesome! By which I mean:

1. I once complimented a contemplator; that was a bad idea. Still, I'll miss the condensational cubed fire pole he gave me in thanks
2. Compliments are the opposite of boobs yet both are awesomeness. The lesson is, if you compliment someone on their boobs and they turn out to be a guy, it's probably not a compliment at all
3. Compliments are like mirrors; if you give them to yourself like I do, you're probably, um sorry, um me me me me me, I mean, you may be narcissistic
4. If you compliment a complimenter and they compliment you back, it creates a compliment one-upmanship encounter that can destroy the world and make you feel really good
5. I hate other people's boyfriends and their bad hearts.

I'M FINALLY READY TO
TALK ABOUT THIS

Speaking of my beautiful, generous and loving heart, I must admit, I am afraid of marriage. That's some hardcore commitment for someone like me. One thing many people don't think about is that the reason women traditionally carried a bouquet of flowers while getting married was because in the olden days people only bathed several times a year, and the flowers were to cover the smell. It's a similar and equally romantic reason we surround the coffin with flowers at a funeral. So there you go, girls, if you want your man to buy you flowers more often you should consider ceasing all bathing activities or killing yourself.

My point is, as humans we like traditions; holidays, anniversaries, rituals, and things we do because that's how people do it. I don't like this. I always want to find the next thing. I like to evolve, develop and create. I've always been that way. That's why I've always hated Shakespeare. In my younger days it was probably mostly because of the annoying olde-worlde language that caused us as kids to totally miss the fact he often wrote delicious smutty tales of kings who want to pork their mothers, but even in this phase I also didn't understand how or why we would let new talent be ignored while people who even claim to love the arts are wasting time on four-hundred-year-old plays that have already been produced thousands upon thousands of times. Let's try something new, for God's sake!

On the other hand, I've always loved girls. I have a special skill whereby their lovely bumpy bits never fail to draw me back to the loving arms of their bosom metaphorically, no matter how many times they treat me like crap.

So, I was in New York a while back planning on setting up a new home. And I was on my way to an improv class at the *Upright Citizens Brigade* when I saw this girl approaching the same building.

'Oh wow, please be in my class!' I pleaded to God and her and myself.

'If this girl had a slightly bigger head she could be a model!' I sweetly thought while perving at her once it turned out she was in my class.

'You better be careful, that's your second one of those today' she said to me two nights later, when we were at the same show, and she saw me purchase a Red Bull, and by saying this, she had just given me a tiny clue that she had noticed me, and had perhaps taken an interest.

'Please, please, please like me', I thought.

And she did! Despite sporting really long, fluorescent colored purple-and-blue hair at the time, which made most people think I was a psycho. Wow. And I liked her. Plus, she didn't even need a bigger head; she WAS a model, a lingerie model even (for the record it was her turtle neck making her head seem small).

Within a month we were packing up her Saab ready to drive across country and move to LA together, despite her hearing my losing my virginity story the first time I did stand-up comedy. I'd never made even a fiftieth of that much of a commitment to a girl before. Less than six weeks after we met we signed a one-year lease together. At this stage, my longest ever relationship was less than six weeks.

Plus, when we were driving across country she slept beside me as I pulled into a small town for dinner and when I asked her what she wanted to eat, before looking up she asked, 'Is there a Denny's?' and I thought 'hang on to this one'. Sometimes it's just meant to be.

Nearly a year and a half later, I found myself stuck in Australia with no visa to return to America. We had been stuck apart for three months and I was desperate to get back to her.

America had warned me from using another tourist visas, as I had abused them for too long, so I needed another type of visa. I knew for sure that I didn't want to be an actor, but as it turned out applying to acting school would get me a student visa and get me back to her. So I signed up. And I sent them a huge chunk of money.

A day before I was due to return to America she broke up with me. Upon my return I was to discover she'd also been cheating on me (in her defense she says she didn't, and yet they celebrate their anniversary two months before we broke up! I hate traditions) and had now left me for the other guy. She had neglected to tell me about the other guy because in her love for me she didn't want me to stop paying all her rent and bills, as I had been for a while. She literally asked me if I would continue to do so as she was breaking up with me. And I said yes! She really was a sweetie. I am still hurt by this, yet the truth is we knew from the beginning, she wanted marriage and kids, and I did not, I hate traditions.

Six months of acting class in LA while nursing a badly broken heart turned out to be really fun, hard, enlightening, and helped me grow as a person. And also constantly reminded me that while I love to perform, I really did not want to be an actor.

Then, one day, right as I was feeling it was time to move on from the school, as part of class I found myself on Santa Monica Boulevard in the heart of Hollywood forced to scream a Shakespeare monologue from *Much Ado About Nothing* with a task of projecting louder than the traffic.

'Shall quips and sentences and these paper bullets of the brain awe a man from the career of his humor? NO! THE WORLD MUST BE PEOPLED!'

Now that's some solid acting!

And I LOVED it. Oh acting, so much fun. I wish I could make a career as an actor. When I was falling in love with my ex we'd run around New York then across America and around LA making a complete idiots of ourselves. It was the most fun I'd ever had. But since then I'd long completely forgotten the joy of making a total fool of myself in public, and of just letting go and not caring what people think! Even as I bellowed my monologue and a guy in a pick-up truck honked his horn and cheered at me it only made me scream louder, to increase the beautiful shame! And it left me feeling ready to be me again. *Intentional* embarrassment is such a different and wonderfully more awesome feeling than that embarrassment which has been thrust upon you.

I still hate Shakespeare, but I was given a big reminder that happiness can sometimes come from the least expected places.

Oh, I also still love the girls, despite how poorly they often seem to treat me.

AND NOW, OFT FORGOTTEN BENEFITS OF A BAD BREAK UP By Dave:

- Reduces clutter in your house – you know, because you smash lots of stuff
- Lots of crying leads to dehydration which is a perfect excuse to go drinking
- If you don't end up murdering someone feeling this bad, you can be pretty sure you never will feel bad enough to kill someone
- If you do end up murdering someone, you can blame your ex
- You get to find out just how hard you need to punch your walls to either break your hand or wall (I recommend wall – unless you're renting)
- Your buddies will all agree that your old girlfriend's teddy bears were kind of gay decorations, and that your new display of teddy bears nailed through the head to the tree in the front yard is way more badass
- Um, hello, obvious one, next time you get laid you get to go back to condoms, awesome!

- Romantic love songs still suck, but now for a DIFFERENT reason
- Perfect opportunity to re-measure your penis and hope for a miracle, therefore re-connecting you with the miracle-giving God you had recently declared couldn't possibly exist and allow you to feel this bad, awww
- Even Shakespeare seems better than reality

WAY BACK WHEN

Then again, maybe *I am* Jim Morrison; or possibly Jesus or Johnny Depp.

Jim Morrison, Jesus and Johnny Depp are the only 'celebrities' that people have consistently told me I kind of sort of a little bit look like, mostly I guess because we are the only four males in history who have ever had long hair.

Could I be Jim Morrison? It would make sense, because recently some friends of mine were watching a documentary about The Doors, and both said something eerie was happening, until they both claim to have independently realized that they were seeing *me* in Jim Morrison's eyes. Also when I was in Paris I picked up a book of Jim Morrison's poetry in the famously awesome Shakespeare Book Co. (wow, I do love that Shakespeare) and my mind nearly exploded. I had never read his poetry before, but reading it now I discovered it was so similar in style and mood to my own poetry that I felt that if someone had told me that I had written those poems I wouldn't doubt them one bit. Plus it would explain why some people argue that he wasn't actually much of a poet. Maybe I am Jim, and maybe that's what drew me to move to LA, and why I randomly started writing crappy poetry at about exactly the age he died?

Let's play a little game of Jim Morrison vs. Dave Tieck

Jim – Born in Melbourne, Florida
Dave – Born in Sydney, Australia

Jim – Known for his gorgeous long wavy hair

Dave – Known for his gorgeous long wavy hair

Jim – Was so shy in his early career he sang with his back to the crowd

Dave – Was so shy in his teenage years he used to create catchphrases and say nothing but those for months on end to save him from thinking of things to say, these included, 'Not really', 'Not definitely' and 'Well, something like that, it all depends on the size of the gap.' (This seriously represents over a year of my conversational skills).

Jim – Had a long-term on-off yet passionate although self-destructive love affair with Pamela Courso.

Dave – Has had a long-term on-off yet passionate although self-destructive love affair with porn.

See, we're basically the same person, hmm, although Jim had charisma, and I missed out on that, hmmm.

Or maybe I am Jesus, or perhaps his probable first incarnation - Adam. I have had some mild doses of stigmata, I have a small scar on the back of my right hand, and I don't know how I got it, and for months at a time I'll develop little wounds on the palm of my hands that never seem to heal. Also God supposedly took a rib from Adam and made Eve with it, and well I have a weird gap in my ribs on my right-hand side, as if someone (that someone being God, is what I'm hinting at there) had taken a rib and, you know, made woman from it. Plus, just like Jesus, I can predict the future sometimes (check this out: In 2025, humans will still use air as our primary source of oxygen—that prediction seriously just came to me). Also, just like Jesus, I can fly! It's only in my dreams for now, but I will bring it to the waking world one day, you just watch me.

"Oh my god, is that someone flying up there?"

"Holy shit, Jesus is returning! Wait, no, that's just David Tieck, boo. Unless, um, has he been Jesus all along?"

Hmmm, then again, I once had an audition to play Jesus and it turned out I was too fat, hmmm.

I was probably never Johnny Depp, because he's been alive all my life, plus when people say that I look like him, it's usually using statements such as 'you look like a less attractive Johnny Depp' or 'you might be trying to look like Johnny Depp but you're just not good looking enough'. So to be him I'd have to be schizophrenic, with two bodies, and a whole lot of friends who are good liars. I have been known to say that my dream girl is one with *reverse* schizophrenic – one awesome personality and multiple bodies, so that makes sense now, but most of my friends are crappy liars while saying mean untruths like 'reverse schizophrenia doesn't exist'. Hmmm, then again I do look gorgeous with my face painted white, and it's way easier to pull off being two people at once when you can fly! Also Johnny Depp *narrated* that Doors documentary, hmmm.

If this year I hope to find out who I really am, maybe I need to figure out who I have *already* been. That's why I decided to go to past-life regression therapy and find out just who, if anyone, I used to be, and what was so messed up in their lives that I brought it back with me in this life to fix.

So I made an appointment, and my far more skeptical friend Faith drove me over, and upon discovering that this would be held in a private apartment rather than an office of some description, she began to fear that not only is past-life stuff a load of crap, but also that I may be actually murdered (Just like happened to, spoiler alert, Jesus).

I was already nervous about delving so deeply into my subconscious; given the excessive violence in many of my dreams, I *know* there are dark demons in there, and I was worried that letting them pass into my conscious mind would turn me into a serial killer. And now I had the fear of *being* the one killed compounding all that. So, for protection, I let Faith walk me to the door. I take nothing but the strictest precautions when lives are at risk!

Once I got inside, it all seemed pretty legit, and my much younger and much handsomer than expected therapist took me into his apartment, which was clearly decorated to suggest warmth and comfort, with natural and earthy color tones, and lots of switched on yet low wattage lamps (the same trick Jim Morrison used to bed women), and he sat me down in a big comfy chair, next to a pile of books on past-life regression, and one fun little doozy about NAZI doctors, and proceeded to do something I wasn't at all prepared for.

He offered me therapy!

I know! That 'therapy' word in his business title about past-life regression therapy is actually what it says it is. We spent a good hour and a half talking about all the bad things that have ever happened to me. Relationship problems, childhood problems, my frequent dreaming of the apocalypse, fears and hates, and things I don't like about myself, and another huge dose of whining that the girls I like don't like me, and ultimately getting me to admit to myself that the truth is that I often think people are judging me and thinking to themselves 'that guy is pathetic' when the truth is what is really going on when I am thinking these thoughts is that I am looking at myself through their eyes and calling myself pathetic. It was a self- realization I needed, and yet still not at all what I was hoping or expecting to achieve here.

'Wow, you used to be Jim Morrison! It took him a while to step into his adored charismatic true self, but trust me, you'll find that in this life too' was what I wanted him to say. Instead, I realized I regard my own self as pathetic. Hmmm, that was kind of the opposite.

As I learned, the way this form of therapy works is that it enables us to look into our past; in this life and others, and even our time spent in the womb (a place Johnny Depp never was, he was gestated in the dreams of unicorns), and significantly any time we've spent unconscious in our lives, and find what negative messages we've had implanted in our minds that we have never acknowledged and let pass on.

We started with hypnosis, a period where I would remain awake and conscious, yet in a deep state of relaxation, and where I was instructed to allow my first thoughts to be acknowledged and explored after a number of questions by him. We regressed to a period in my childhood when I was being scolded for failing a school exam, and where I had made a conscious choice to continue to fail rather than allow being yelled at to work as a way to motivate me.

I'd forgotten all about doing that. It turns out that numerous times in my childhood I honestly made the decision to *own* failing on my terms, rather than let punishment have a positive effect on my life. At the time, this was my way of seeking to control my own destiny. They also call it cutting off your nose to spite your face, or also being a total jagoff moronic tardlike idiot.

By picturing myself in this moment making a more positive response to my punishment, I was supposed to be able to relieve myself of the guilt of making these poor decisions in the first place. I don't know if it worked, but as we began to put aside this memory, I felt light, so light I almost felt like I was about to float out of the chair. (Fly yet, Dave? Nope, but damn close, David!)

He now asked me to tell him the very next thing I thought of. I have no idea why, but the next thing I thought about was sitting in a chair in a dressing room, one of those ones you see in movies with lights all around the mirror. I was looking into the mirror and staring back at me was a woman, a young woman putting her make-up and clothes on in preparation to go on stage, and more than that, preparing her mind to face the audience.

This, if you believe this sort of thing, was me in a past life. I am skeptical of things like this. I have always been of one of those naysayers who point out that there are as many people alive right now as the rest of the time of human existence combined, so it is impossible for us all to have had past lives.

I am also opened minded and a dreamer. The dreamer in me likes the idea of this stuff being true. That we get lots of chances at this game of life, and get to experience it all, but with the one drawback that we don't get to take our knowledge and experience with us to the next life. At least not consciously.

I don't know if I want it to be true. I love the thought that by opening myself up to this that I may find a quicker path to be the man I wish to be. But I am not sure it is worth it. What I do know is this: I have never ever sat and imagined myself as a woman in an old theater dressing room before.

We began to delve into her life, with me talking as her in the first person. I was about to go on stage. I knew they were going to praise me, as they always did, but I hated that they didn't know that deep down I didn't feel love. Praise is not love. I wanted people to know that the real me had feelings, and hurt sometimes, and felt sad sometimes. Instead I was always only shown off as having it all, the perfect life. The tears hidden from my adoring public.

As we delved into my life I was to discover I was in a serious relationship, but it was a sham, my partner/fiancé/husband and I were only ever together when we were in public, and I didn't know anything about him. I wanted real love, but I owed the people who had made me a star, and had to do what they told me or else risk losing it all and being left with nothing.

As I entered her mind, my body began to twitch, especially my legs. I could not control this at all, and tried to ignore it at first, but it was strong and pronounced. Even while trying to fight it, the twitches changed the position of my legs. My knees moved together, and my feet moved to face inwards. My body had physically moved into a more feminine way of holding itself.

Now we began to talk about my current life, and how these feeling may be affecting my current mental state. To me it is obvious. My current sub-conscious is worried that if I build that persona, the one she took on stage, that the same pattern will happen and I will be unable to feel love on a personal individual basis.

As we talked about me in the present, completely against my physical will my mind twitched my body back to a masculine stance. We would go in and out of her for a while and each time my body would twitch and move from masculine to feminine and back on its own. No matter how much I tried to control or fight it, it was fruitless.

I don't know if it was a past life or if it was problems in my current sub-conscious inventing a past-life story that would explain some of my current idiosyncrasies, but I do know that I was not intentionally inventing anything. David Tieck and *her* definitely had some differences of thought and opinion. I don't know how to explain it; it was just a 'feeling'.

Then we moved on to her death.

Current-day David Tieck has often foreseen himself dying in a car crash with himself at the wheel. I do not like to drive and when I do, I do it with the strongest sense of safety in mind. I've had some lucky breaks on the road; a couple of times I had brief micro-sleeps at the wheel and didn't crash, and I don't know if this has affected me, but some voice in the back of my head tells me that if I keep driving it will kill me eventually, so I don't.

When the therapist asked me to move to the moment of her death, the first thought that came to my mind was me, as her, at the wheel with the car spinning out of control. And me, as her, making the decision not to try to fight the car back into control but rather think of my life and decide to let the crash happen. Not quite suicide, but not fighting to live.

David Tieck would not do this. She did. David Tieck is scared of dying like this. She almost welcomed it. According to the therapist, at the moment of our death in past lives we take stock and basically choose to take our dissatisfaction into the next life, hoping to make up for our mistakes. This thought process leads to us repeating patterns until we fix them.

He asked me to go into her mind just after death and feel how she felt, and I felt like she immediately deeply regretted her decision not to fight in that moment, and subsequently fight for what she had truly wanted her whole life. Did my current fears of not fighting for what I want in life and dying in a car crash find birth at her death, or did my current feelings on this manifest this story? I don't know. It's chicken and egg stuff. What I do know is that as I came out of the hypnosis I found myself inspired and fired up to better myself.

I had joked around beforehand about the fallacy of everyone who has past lives always finding famous past lives and I maintained the cliché. Although perhaps only those with interesting past lives are motivated to seek these answers? Or is it merely humans' fame whoring yearnings?

Then I realized that this meant I could prove this to be true or not. She was a famous actress who died in a car crash while at the wheel. If this woman existed there would be records of her life and death. So I jumped online and tried to find her, but I have not found her as of yet. In the regression I felt like she was possibly in New York and it was around the 1920s, but this information was never specified, and for some reason I feel that perhaps she was in France, or Russia, and I haven't looked into her deeply enough yet. Part of me doesn't want to know.

What I do know, on the other hand, is this. Evolution works by making subtle changes in offspring, which if prove valuable or advantageous, can help such animal thrive and reproduce. For example, at one point in the transition from primate to human we did not have opposable thumbs. A child was born at one point with this anomaly and he found it valuable and so bred well and passed it on to subsequent generations. At one point there was a species, which was an ancestor to the chicken, and one of these ancestors one day laid an egg which contained an animal with enough differences to make it no longer the ancestor species but now a chicken. The egg came before the chicken, the chicken came before the chicken egg, and any scientist who can't work this out is a total jagoff moronic tardlike idiot.

Also, I know I want the idea of past lives to be true, 'cause if it is then there is still a chance I was Jim Morrison.

Also, if I was a centipede in a past life, I really, really hope that I wasn't in the mafia. I mean, what if I was sent off to break some dude's kneecap? How the hell would you choose **which** kneecap? That's the kind of hellish decision that would make me kill myself in a centipede car crash, or at least not do everything to live.

PLEASE DON'T HONK AT ME

My teenage years weren't ALL bad. When I was 17 I got my driver's license! At this time I still looked like I was nine or ten, and so despite scoring a hundred percent on my driving test (I nearly lost a point for going too slow at one point) and despite being an obsessively safe driver, I was pulled over by the police constantly. I didn't receive my first ticket for a driving offense until I was in my twenties, but in the first three years of driving I must have been pulled over thirty times.

From what I understand, the police were not allowed to pull a car over on suspicion of an underage driver, so they had to come up with other excuses for why they stopped me. I would often get told I had a brake light out, only to prove that it wasn't, or I'd get told I had gone close to breaking some road rule that I hadn't broken, and one time a cop said he pulled me over just to ask if I knew the football score! On a more fateful day, I was pulled over under the guise of 'this car matches the description of a stolen car' and to maintain the ruse, the two cops told me they needed to search my car.

Small problem. My trunk was full of X-rated porn, which, while it had been purchased legally, at the time it was illegal to possess it in my state. I sat in the front seat of my car for what seemed to be an hour, while watching in the review mirror as two cops looked through my ample porn collection. In hindsight, they were probably just enjoying looking at the pictures on the covers and making jokes about how the driver's voice hadn't even broken yet so what the hell was he going to do with a big pile of porn. But in the moment I was convinced I was going to be humiliatingly arrested, with my image shown all over news with the heading 'THE PRE-PUBESCENT PORN MERCHANT – CAPTURED!' Thank God porn has since moved its residence over to the Internet so perverts like me can self-loathe without the public fanfare.

In the end, the police officers, in an out of tradition act of decency, admitted that he had pulled me over without a probable cause and therefore would let me go with a warning on the porn. It all worked out in the end, but it was mortifyingly terrifying and embarrassing at the time. I should point out I also had a friend in the car with me, and up until then he had no idea I owned that much porn.

We drove off in silence, with me, as usual, following every road rule to the absolute letter, knowing I would get pulled over again very soon regardless, and not at all enjoying driving the way other young males all seem to.

In Los Angeles, when a car is turning left at an intersection with four-way traffic lights and on-coming traffic is flowing, after the light changes for said on-coming traffic, one car is allowed to run the red or the end of the orange to make their left turn. *One* car is allowed, yet three *always* go.

When I am driving, I cannot bring myself to break this rule, as I am still a stickler for road rules, unlike seemingly everyone else in the city. I think they're there for a reason. In this case it's dangerous to make this turn, pedestrians are often still crossing and the cars have already received their green light to start moving from the other direction, and these law breakers always rush through as fast as possible, quite often clearly not taking all the precautions necessary to maintain safety for all around them.

I can't do it, I won't do it and I shouldn't do it. And when I don't do it, the car behind honks at me *always*. Honked at for my refusal to break the law and prioritizing safety and my fellow man rather than a selfish need to be wherever I am going. This is what the world has become? It makes me angry, it makes me feel embarrassed knowing people are looking at me like *I'm* the bad guy, it makes me upset with the human race so much that I want to cry (other things on the road do this to me too, honking cars or tailgating them for *only* going the speed *limit,* thinking the right on red rule means you don't even have to look up to see if a pedestrian is crossing on *their green* light, the fact that almost every single person you meet turns into a completely selfish, impatient, dangerous asshole the second they get behind the wheel. I don't know if there is man made global warming or not, but I do know there is one swift way to reduce the world's pollution and reliance on oil, and that is to simply strip the drivers licenses of all the people who clearly show they do not take the responsibility as seriously as it needs to be taken). I regularly have premonitions that I am going to die in car crashes. In a past life I may have already died in a car crash. Yet the *reason* I drive as little as humanly possible is because people honk at you for not breaking the law.

They're being mean to me, and I don't like meanies. And I also don't like breaking rules. I don't know why, I just don't, ok? I hate conforming, I hate tradition, and yet I hate breaking rules. I'm a self-hating stickler. And yes I know that sticklers are awesome. I mean obviously, like whenever I am at a party I just burst in, find the host, and say 'point me out the sticklers, I want to stick by them ALL NIGHT!' But I don't want to be one, and end up like the politically correct, spelling Nazi, seek negative when it need not be sought people, so ok, run down pedestrians if you must, but please don't honk your horns at me, it really hurts my feelings.

So, is this an embarrassing memory I need to murder? Hell no. Why? Because I have rolling around in my memory my period of being such a badass that my crime spree of passion didn't end till I was arrested! Yep, this kid has done some wrong. I done some hardcore wrong.

Here is the scene: I had recently purchased a new pump to pump up my various sporting balls. I had a lot of balls - rugby balls, soccer balls, touch football balls, American football balls, basketballs, tennis balls and cricket balls, and although tennis balls and cricket balls don't actually need to be pumped up, the others all frequently did.

Thanks to my new pump, my balls were all nearly once again full of air, firm, and nice to the touch and bounce, but before I had finished my job I snapped the needle. I went to the store where I had purchased the pump a couple of days later and tried to find a replacement needle, only to find out THEY DIDN'T EXIST!

THIS was OUTRAGEOUS! Anyone who has ever used one of these pumps knows that you go through a lot of needles per pump. Most pumps give you a replacement at the time of purchase KNOWING you will break them. But this store, K-Mart for the record, was essentially selling you a car, knowing the wheels would soon need replacing, and knowing that they were irreplaceable! Those bastards!

I had to take a stand. I know what they wanted me to do, purchase another pump and be on my pissed-off way, but I wasn't willing to do that, there was a principle at stake. And so I did what any man would do, I stood up for the right of the people and tried to steal a replacement needle from one of the other pumps that was for sale.

I used my excellent sleuth skills and looked around nervously for about an hour, then slowly undid a package, and slid the needle into my wallet.

Next thing I know I am being hauled into the security office. Seems an undercover security guard had been watching me the whole time. Seriously, Kmart had an undercover security guard, probably earning $50 an hour, watching me for an hour to stop me stealing a needle that would have cost about $1.99 if they carried it.

Then they had me drilled by a crack team of three or four investigators in a back security office for well over an hour about what the hell was my problem, and why did I have to be a meany and steal, while I told them it was the principle, and they were like, 'Why not just buy another pump?' and I was like, 'I already said it's the principle, you fucking retards.' By the way, I had a friend for a while who stole thousands of dollars worth of products from this exact store around this time. He stole videos, he would put on clothes and wear them out of the store, and he even stole a remote-control car, one piece at a time! I used to think he was doing something very wrong, until I met the team of security who had collectively probably cost the company hundreds of dollars in wages to try and stop a pathetically shy fifteen-year-old stand up for himself for the first time in years.

Failing to get me to crack and admit that I was actually a vicious lifetime store thief, they banned me from the store for a year, and called the cops.

The cop came to take me away, and walking out with him I felt as mortified as I ever had. I tried to make it look like, rather than being arrested, I was being picked up by my dad, so I started talking to him like we'd known each other for years. It was the most inspired talking I did all decade. It didn't work at all, people looked at me like I was dirt. 'Another kid throwing his life away'.

I spent another couple of hours in the police station copping the same interrogation. Again, I don't think he believed for a second that I was doing it out of principle. But at least the taxpayers got their money's worth that day. By the way, since I grew my hair long, I meet drug dealers every day, as they all come up to me all the time assuming I am a user, even though I never touch drugs. So, me someone who wants to avoid drug dealers as much as possible can't help finding them, yet the cops can't find them? Too busy interrogating scared-to-death fifteen year olds standing up for themselves for once.

I still rarely stand up for myself. I deflect. I use humor as a defense and try to joke my way out of things. I internalize, and I cry. I just take what's worse for me rather than say what's right for me. I hate conflict. I hate drama. I hide from them all as much as possible. But I should stand up for myself a little bit.

Then again, one time I did send a long angry letter to Coca Cola completely abusing them for their cruel cancellation of the sale of Cherry Coke in Australia. When there is a cause I *believe* in, I'll be strong. I was furious and promised deep anger-induced retribution. I even made this hate-filled declaration: 'I will now consume fewer Coca Cola products.' Take that, evil corporation. I even kept it up for a day or so!

Plus, I am not a total goody-two-shoes these days. In fact, just the other day I was walking down a quiet street late at night and after carefully looking around to make sure no one could see me, with my heart pounding in my chest, and my throat swallowing heavily, I totally J-walked. Take that, long arm of the law!

FUCK YOU (I'M ONLY SAYING THAT IN CASE IT CURES ME)

Truth is, I've always been my own worst enemy. The morning after my recent girlfriend broke up with me, I woke up with a huge bruise on my right butt cheek. I consulted my book of do-it-yourself remedies and a day later jumped on a plane from Sydney to Los Angeles, and shockingly, rather than curing it, fifteen hours of a high-pressured atmosphere while sitting down letting every bit of blood possible congregate in my ass meant that within forty-eight hours or so my ass looked like a giant had stepped on Prince (for photographic evidence please look me up online, of the bruise, that is—I don't have those pictures of Prince right now, but if anyone knows any giants, I am hiring).

A couple of days later I woke up in the middle of the night during a horrible nightmare and found myself punching the living crap out of my leg.

'Davey did a whoopsie.'

Ahh, the source of my mysterious morning bruises had finally been identified: I *do* punch myself while sleeping! Also during this period, while sleepwalking during nightmares, I found myself getting online and tweeting such vile, anger-riddled messages that my friends started to worry that I needed to be put on suicide watch, and Satan called me up and asked me to tone it down for the sake of his reputation. (He's the bashful type, Satan, that's why his cheeks are always so rosy red).

What I am trying to get at is that a couple of months ago I woke up and mysteriously had a sore jaw. After a couple of weeks my gums in that area began to get inflamed and I thought I had a dental issue. It felt like a wisdom tooth coming in, and as I had already had all mine removed, I spent a couple of days boasting I was so wise I need extra (hey, I get shit done while sleeping, that's a sign of wisdom if you ask me) and made a dentist appointment. He shot me down and said I wasn't so wise after all and to start flossing, you tool, and since then I have tried every remedy in the book to fix this jaw. I've tried massaging it, I've tried resting it, I've tried wishing it would go away, I've tried whining and *none* of it works. The medical profession has failed me again.

I talked about this with my past-life regression therapist when I saw him and he said something I had actually thought of myself; my sore jaw might be my body's way of telling me that I am not saying something I should be, rather than me head butting kitchen appliances while I am asleep.

I can't think what the hell this could be. I say all sorts of things no one should ever say, but I can't think for the life of me of what I should be saying but am not.

Earlier today I was eating fast food for a change in my regular routine of eating fast food, and I ran into a friend I hadn't seen in ages and right away he said, 'Damn man, what have you been doing to put on all that weight?'

'Fuck you,' is what I should have said, but instead I got all depressed and went and cried my way through a couple of hours in the gym. And in the gym I had an epiphany!

'What is stuff you nearly say, but then don't say, Dave?'

'I don't know, David, but you just asked that like it was some sort of rhetorical question in which case just frigging answer it yourself, you cryptic bastard.'

'I was trying to do a slow reveal, Dave, you know, to build suspense or tension or something. What's wrong with that?'

'Because, David, now you have built it up too much and if it doesn't live up to it, we're going to look like a fool.'

'Don't worry about that, Dave, this ain't going to disappoint anyone. Check this out, dude: sometimes, from time to time, we write shit we're thinking of tweeting and then we hold off, but keep it in our cell phone draft box.'

'That is genius, David, of course! That's what we're not saying that perhaps we should be saying!'

So, if you will allow it, my friends Dave and David would now like to reveal some of the things I think yet choose *not* to say, in the hopes it'll fix my jaw.

- I believe in an eye for a testicle; if you accidently poke your eye out with a fork you should punish yourself by poking out a testicle, or else you'll just go blind and it's gay to be that silly.
- I have decided to abjure from consuming cheeseburgers until the other ingredients get just as much credit for the deliciousness as the cheese. It's about equality, you racists.
- Did you ever wish someone would give you some soap and they don't, so you get all pissed off and jump up on your soapbox to complain but then you're like, 'Oh, I already have a whole box of soap'?
- If you have awful taste in music I recommend you start listening to it and stop licking it, you weirdo.
- I wonder if any girl has ever tried to hide cash in her vagina so it won't be stolen and then a guy tried to rape her and was like, 'Ah yeah, two birds with one stone.' I really hope not, I hate that saying, it's so unnecessarily violent.
- Do you ever think that the homeless would be more likely to seek help or make an effort to change if we were all like, 'Yo hobo, what's the down lo mo' fo?' I hope so, getting to yell that out in public all the time would be awesome.

- I've had more sexual partners than most people have had gangrene limbs they have had to cut off their own bodies with plastic spatulas, so suck on that.
- I think we'd all be happier if we could just control concrete. I recommend staring at it meanly, which will mess with its self-esteem hardcore.

I could keep going for a long time. I have many thoughts like these, but I shouldn't reveal all the crazy till I find out if this works! So now that I have said that, I hope if I wake up with a bruise on my ass tomorrow it looks more like a giant has stepped on a beautiful lady.

Results: A day later no butt bruise and jaw still sore. Maybe I should try revealing something I thought about the people around me.

- In Trader Joe's today and discovered their meatless meatballs. Hey, vegetarians, if you don't want to eat meat then meatballs aren't for you! I disagree with wearing spiders as hats, but there ain't no spiderless spider hats at Trader Joe's.
- To the girl who has obliterated her body and face with excessive plastic surgery who was going on and on about finding 'good organic coffee', just for saying that I should poke your implants open with a rusty knife and let you chemical bleed to death.
- Sometimes when I shop I get overwhelmed with emotion by the cute baby ducks on the toilet paper. I hope that doesn't come out in any negative ways, like wanting to kill poor plastic girls or anything.

Results: Jaw still sore. I'm going to put my mind back in its proper place again, in the fairy land it lives in full of teddy bears and serial killers. It's happier there; in that world Satan is pink, plus free soap for everyone.

'CAUSE, YOU KNOW

Speaking of speaking, high school is often a wonderful time for people. My school had a unique element to it. I went to a private Anglican school with a rich history as an all-boys school for over a hundred years. However, in an effort to increase the number of students (to get more money) they jumped onto the unique idea that the parents of girls could also afford to pay hugely expensive private school fees for the same poor level of education as us boys were enjoying. So the decision was made to start allowing girls to attend the school.

It was too big a task to co-ed up all ten years of schooling they provided, so at first they allowed girls to attend only in the last two years of high school. Thus it was for my 165-odd classmates, as we were entering the most important two years of our schooling life, the ones where they drum into you that your entire future depends on, for the first time in our lives they offered the distraction of boobs, 200 of them, or 100 girls, just enough to make sure even if every single girl hooked up with a boy 65 of us would be left out in the cold.

It was a wondrous time. Overnight, the personality of every single boy changed completely. People I had known since we were ten suddenly went from funny to serious, or from quiet to attempting to be funny, or weirdly mean, or obsessed with their hair, or obsessed with their pimples to the point of poking them till they exploded in class (at that time I personally only ever *dreamed* of getting a pimple, but when I started getting four thousand a day as a 23 year old I regretted some of these teenaged dreams). Everyone changed in some way. For years there had been cliques, and groups of friends, and this natural order was thrown into all-out chaos, as the goals had now all moved. Now there were girls, things were getting interesting.

As couples began to form, guys began to tell stories of girls who had let them finger out their vaginas, and my shyness took an acute turn from horrendous to off-the-charts ghastly. It was unspeakably bad—literally. As the only boy in the year that I knew of to still be a good two years away from the onset of puberty, shorter than ALL of the girls, looking nine years old, having got really fat seemingly all of a sudden, and unable and unwilling to fit in with the trends, my confidence with the boobs who had now shown up was clearly not even at the very back of the disgusting mess which was my locker. This was not helped by the fact that one of the key factors boys need to have luck with the ladies, at any age, is strong wingmen, and I was a paper plane that had been dropped in a used toilet compared to the other full-grown penises flying fighter jets. By the end of the first year, I believe, as far as school was concerned I was a borderline mute.

I didn't speak unless asked a question, and the rare times that happened I mostly gave one-word answers, even to questions like, 'What do you think about the Economics assignment we had to do over the weekend?'

'No,' I'd reply.

At times people would literally ask me to go away. 'If you're not going to say anything, just go away' they would say, and unable to think of anything to say for a couple of excruciatingly awkward minutes, I would get up and leave.

Later I would develop the pre-mentioned 'not really', 'not definitely' and 'well, something like that, it all depends on the size of the gap' (I think I stole this one from a rap song, which just adds to the sadness) as catchphrases so I would at least get more than the odd 'yes' and 'no' out. If someone said to me something that I could not think of a response to, I would simply say one of these three things.

'Going to the party this weekend?'

'Not definitely.'

'Do you think you did well on the test?'

'Not really.'

'Oh my God, those bushfires burning all those people's houses down last summer was so sad, wasn't it?'

'Not definitely'

'Are you mentally handicapped?'

'Well, something like that, it all depends on the size of the gap.'

But even ingenuity such as this did not propel me into becoming a confident speaker. By the end of our two years with girls I barely had a friend at school left, and managed to go the entire time without having a single conversation with a girl. That's how cool I am!

When you don't ever talk, there is something else that becomes prominent in your life—watching. This was the biggest period in my life for merely observing human behavior. And having done this, having had the unique experience of observing a controlled experiment where 165 boys were trapped in an environment with no members of the opposite sex, and then one day introducing 100 girls into said environment, I was able to study the behavior from the inside, the mute who after a while became invisible to them. I am basically like that woman with those gorillas in that mist. And from this study, and subsequent ones, I believe I have earned the right to coin a word that should be in the dictionary damn it.

When 165 16- and 17-year-old boys get introduced to 100 16- and 17-year-old girls who will be part of their lives for the next two years on the same day, hormones, I guess you would say, do pump. On this day, crushes are formed, future husbands meet their future wives, and I learned something I was not expecting: The ones you take an instant liking to, even from afar, are not the ones the superficial male in you who reads porn obsessively would go for first. Even without a word spoken, and the girls all dressed in the same uniforms, our brains make unconscious judgments about the type of a person they are. We are not just attracted to attractiveness. Clearly something else is going on.

All sorts of studies have been done over the years trying to prove the existence of pheromones, or that men unconsciously seek a woman with a good figure for giving birth, or that women are attracted to broad shoulders because their ancestors saw that as a key to fighting off dinosaurs and time travellers and all that, and some of these things may be true, but what they never point out is what exactly they say we are feeling when we have these thoughts.

We talk about lust, and then we take a huge leap to love at first sight. When we see someone for the first time, someone we find attractive, but on a deeper level than lust, something that tells us that this person is supposed to be in our lives for some reason, but with far too much still to be known before we can call it love, we experience a wonderful feeling I call 'lavid'. I named it after a guy named David, myself, giving it a 'l' to keep it in the family with lust and love (I've been pushing this word for years and it only just occurred to me that naming a word about a feeling of extreme attraction you find in another human after yourself is kind of narcissistic, but then again if you can't love yourself no one else will. Oh, also buy my next book, *How to be a Narcissist* you'll find it in the *self*-help section).

Lavid can lead to love, but it often doesn't. Lavid has elements of lust, but it's better. Sometimes you see someone from afar and instantly just 'know' this person is supposed to be in your life in some way or another—that's Lavid lovely people! Lavid is powerful, it's sweet, it's tender, it's beautiful, and needs to be recognized. So please send angry letters to your local *Webster's* editor today.

While we're correcting vastly despicable flaws in the dictionary, there is something else that should be pointed out. 'Orange', 'Silver', 'Month' and 'Purple have been coasting along like spoiled children arrogantly hanging onto selfish lack of perfect rhyme companion for too goddamn long. It really spoiled my rock song about the month I spent picking oranges when I unfortunately punctured my hand on a loose silver nail leaving my fingers purple and sore really hard to write. So I am going to correct that right now.

NEW WORDS COINED by Dave that rhyme with silver, month, purple and orange:

- Silver: 'Krilver'—if you don't enjoy baths yet keep trying just in case then you're a Krilver
- Month: 'Hunth'—to fear that leaves changing color for autumn will melt your second smallest toe.
- Purple: Cop this, Purple - 'Terple'—if you know you want to eat cheese, but are not sure which variety of cheese, you are Terple!
- Orange: 'Horange' which means to hate people who hate so much that you hate yourself and end up making love to lots of whores.

Done, dictionary fixed and my lack of speaking embarrassments turned into talking so much I am expanding the very ability of all humans to speak! Now, get working, songwriters; life just got a hell of a lot more interesting.

OUT THE BACK OF MY PLACE
IS WHERE FUN HAPPENS

Parties are a great place to meet sexy strangers or maybe find some beautiful lavid with someone rich and famous. Given my acute shyness during high school, it may surprise some of you to know that I threw the biggest party my school, and probably even my neighborhood had ever seen. It was a party so big it was mentioned in the local newspapers. A party I threw! I, a kid who spent most of his lunches reading the newspapers alone in the library, threw a party that *made* the newspapers.

Here is what happened. As the new school year was launched, my parents told me I could have a couple of friends over for a movie night sleep over so I could catch up with kids I hadn't seen all summer. I mentioned this to a couple of friends, who said they would come over, and they mentioned it to a few friends, who mentioned it to a few friends, and two days later over a hundred people asked me if they could also come to the huge party I was throwing that weekend.

Now, I have an IQ which tests up in the high levels of the population (according to an online test I am determined to believe was accurate and not a scam to sell me encyclopedias). And the truth is, despite possessing a very intelligent brain, and endless modesty, I get pissed off anytime I hear of a person with an IQ higher than mine because I hate that this is not something I can better them in. I am an egotistical narcissist at my very core. (Actually, to be honest, I am too damn awesome to be a narcissist!) A lot of people don't actually believe I have a high IQ, because I did awful at school, spent the best part of a decade unable to think of anything to say, and because when I do speak I am prone to saying totally retarded things like, 'Yes, we are having a party.'

In my defense, I started telling people the party was going on for a lot of not party-related reasons. For one thing, when people ask you about your party because they want to party and are told you are having a party, they respond with more happiness when you tell them you *are* having a party than when you tell them you are *not* having a party. I don't like people being unhappy with me, and lying is often a good way to avoid this.

Also, I was the most naive teenager who has ever been alive in the history of the world. There are Mormon kids in the middle of Utah who were caught looking at a picture of a girl on a billboard that was seven miles away when they were twelve so have been locked in a basement for their entire teenage years who are less naive about what teenagers get up to than I was.

Evidence that I was hugely naïve includes these facts:

- It hadn't even occurred to me that *any* 16 or 17 year olds would drink alcohol, and when it was pointed out to me that some may I told my friends to see if they can get them to do it in hiding down under my house where we had a little crawl space that was too filled with spiders for us ever to go near
- It didn't occur to me that letting some of my friends know that my dad kept his wine collection in this space would mean that over the course of the year thousands of dollars of wine would be stolen from my dad (in one case a friend of mine stole a bottle of red wine worth a couple of grand, drank it way too quickly and vomited all over another friend's brand new white carpet in what may well be the world's most expensive ever vomit. I

myself now fantasize about drinking some of that thousand-dollar champagne filled with gold flakes and vomiting on the Mona Lisa at the Louvre in Paris. Only thing stopping me is the long line to get in, I hate long lines!)

- It didn't occur to me that some of these kids might feel confident, or mature enough to try and spend some of this evening trying to do naughty things to members of the opposite sex.

- And it didn't ever for a moment occur to me that the reality was that 16 and 17 year olds would *so* want to get drunk and try to do naughty things to members of the opposite sex that the rumor of my party spread first through my school, then through my suburb, and then all the way up the two main train lines and to all the schools that used them.

Our end-of-year high-school yearbook has a section listing the five best parties thrown during the whole two years we were all together. At the bottom of the list it says: Dave Tiek?

Yes, they spelled my name wrong; no one knew a god damn thing about me. They also put a question mark, because what actually took place was first a massive poster campaign by a friend and I, hoping to redirect the party to a nearby park, where it was estimated something like several thousand teenagers planned to show up to for a party, only to have the cops show up before the sun set, sending revelers running in all sorts of directions, before countless other parties broke out in parks across the neighborhood, dozens of fines were given out for underage drinking, I believe several arrests, and a police force baffled as to why on one particular weekend so many kids had descended on one suburb and tried to have illegal parties in parks. Some of these parties were apparently awesome. And the whole running all over the place and finding scores of drunken teenagers everywhere was apparently shitloads of fun.

I wasn't at any of these other parties. When the cops showed up, I quickly unplugged the tiny tape player I had ridiculously thought could entertain 3000 people and bolted for my house, climbing over the fence leading into the vacant lot behind that was between our house and the park the quickest I had ever done it (finding the best way over this fence had been a battle us kids had fought for years and years, turned out the best way was to be raging with fear), where, petrified that the cops would show up at my place, I lay in the long, years-since-mown, grass that I knew held Sydney funnel webs, the world's deadliest spider, and possibly deadly snakes, both things I was terrified of, and I lay in that grass for probably two hours, the entire time with my heart pumping, and almost shitting myself any time I heard a voice or saw the flash of a car's headlight.

It would be many, many years before I would learn to enjoy going to parties.

Now I party all the time. Too much. Way too much. Sometimes every night of the week. The problem isn't so much the volume of the partying, although that is a problem we'll get to shortly, the problem is the quality. I am in a party rut. Here is what I do: I get all enthusiastic, and then go to a bar or too infrequently a live music venue, planning on having the time of my life, before slowly letting the night wear me away, as I get rejected by scores of girls, see others canoodling in ways I would like to be, get too drunk, and then get pissed off and start sending text messages and tweets that I regret deeply the next morning.

As an experiment, I recently decided to write what I was thinking while making this transformation, in the moment, while ridiculously drunk, as the thoughts were coming to me, in the hope of reading them back later to get a better insight into who exactly I am while in this mindset. Here is the unedited text of what I wrote (The notes in parenthesis are after the thought commentary):

- I used to be able to hold my alcohol like no one else, I could drink copious amounts, never get sick, violent, sloppy, or even a hangover and remember it all. Things are starting to change, goddamn it.

- Now I am horrendously prone to stupid acts, which I regret for a long time after, and worse now I have huge periods blacked out with not a lick of a memory.
- So I am recently heartbroken and in a town where I don't know anyone I can go out drinking with in the hope of meeting girls I can break down crying in front of when I even think of romantic things in her vicinity. There was only one thing for it - I must go out drinking alone. My new experiences in this activity have taught me that I will drink way faster when alone, in lieu of conversation, and after a certain point I will remember little. So this I write in the midst of it, so I find out exactly what sort of things I am thinking.
- I write this right now in a bar full of hot chicks and I am alone. My chances of picking one of them up are 0.0002% (I can't believe I am capable of such optimism when drunk!)
- I am at the level of drunk already where I know I won't remember this has made me realize something, I have just discovered a super power, I can do something nuts right now, or bold, or crazy, and if I am willing to trust the blackout qualities of the booze and I won't remember it, so who cares (why do I feel like I have made this 'discovery' lots of times and just never remember how clearly ludicrous it is?)
- Plus morning after one night stand sex is always the best (how the hell did I just make the leap from maybe I'll do something crazy to I am getting laid, and even though I won't remember it, I can take solace in the fact I can probably go for round two when we wake up?)
- Ok, a really cute girl just approached me and then was instantly horribly upset I was me (Do girls like drunk manic depressives?)
- I feel like I'm inside of the mind of misery right now, time for another drink (shut up you depressing cunt).

- Whbd fucki ng fuck you culnt (surprisingly I woke up alone).

Clearly I need another way. So yesterday my horoscope said to me that all the things I have been working on the past few years are about to start becoming big successes, and that it was so guaranteed I should spend the evening celebrating. I let the seed germinate in my mind and then out to celebrate I went, with a promise to celebrate *everything* that I saw and that happened. And you know what? It was so good that I started making life plans to live like this for every moment forever! Here are some things I wrote down while celebrating.

- I'm at the bar alone and there are some cute girls here, but there is that burlesque show down the road I could also go check out. I think pessimistically for a moment that I bet I make the wrong decision, but then I remember I am supposed to celebrate everything. 'I have choice,' I think, 'that's pretty bloody good, and I remember I am in Hollywood pursuing my dreams, and it's a Friday night, and I am celebrating my future success, and not only am I having fun but my big problem is choosing where to continue having fun, hell yeah! Now I am beaming with smiles
- See a cute girl leaning up against the wall, she looked at me, it wasn't a smile but it was a linger. I should go up and talk to her but I don't have the balls. So instead of getting pissed off at myself, I think, 'Hell yeah, I still have in my future the joy of coming into that confidence, unlike my contemporaries who just go through the routine, or are married and will never get to feel that little spark of 'maybe she'll like me' again, that's worth celebrating.'
- See a girl wearing ridiculously high and uncomfortable high heels, something which I am getting more and more pissed off by, and instead now I think, thank you, you're letting me know from the get go that you are an

idiot, saving me from wasting my time trying to get to know you

- See a girl with big fake boobs, and instead of thinking 'screw you for destroying something I may have found beautiful', I celebrate her for letting me know off the bat that she has an ugly lying soul
- Bus boy drops a cup of ranch dressing on the floor, it explodes and splashes all over me and another guy. I can't help but laugh, I am in too good a mood not to, the other guy's is completely furious and I celebrate the fact that my attitude has made something that he feels anger for bring me to laughter
- I'm standing at the bar and a guy pushes his way into my space forcing me to move, I look at him with a 'what the hell are you doing' stare and he says back in a borderline retarded drawl 'whatever bro' and instead of breaking my beer bottle on his face I think, 'In two seconds that guy let me know I am a smarter and a more decent human than him, and the reality is I am smarter and more decent than most people,' and I move over near some cute girls beaming while I celebrate being who I am.

Those were just a few of the many, many mini-moments of celebration I experienced that night. Some of that may sound a little cynical to you, but that is almost the point. I was celebrating turning my negativity into positivity and it felt really great. This isn't just an experience I want to do for a while to write about, this is how I plan to live the rest of my awesomely celebration worthy life!

And I feel so good about this I might even throw a party to celebrate, and I wouldn't be upset at all of 3000 17 year olds show up!

IS IT WRONG TO MASTURBATE WHILE LOOKING AT A PICTURE OF YOURSELF?

A couple of years ago I was unlucky enough to briefly get to know a steroid-abusing self-absorbed scumbag of the most pathetically high order, after friend of mine moved in with him, for two and half a days, before his psycho ways meant we had to rescue her and move her out at four in the morning.

Within this brief time period, he did a number of things both horrendous and excessively egotistical. These included threatening my friend on numerous occasions in many different ways, to the extent she feared for her physical safety, and also actually physically abusing her cat. He really was a top-notch guy. Top notch on the list of people I would comfortable allow to be incarcerated for a crime they didn't commit (yet).

Also, one time I knocked on his door and he yelled out 'just a minute' and when he finally opened the door he was wearing nothing but boxer briefs, making me realize that when he has someone knock on the door and doesn't know who it is, he uses this time to take clothes *OFF!*

Yet the thing about him that was most disturbing to me was this—the screen saver on his computer was a picture of himself, naked, looking at himself in the mirror. Yes, this is a guy who chooses to constantly *look at himself looking at himself!*

That's just, um, WEIRD!

'Hey me, I see me there, what are you looking at me? Oh me! My oh my, me is gorgeous. Me and me might watch me *all* day, me, I might even watch me watching me watching me.'

I bring this up now because I've spent a fair bit of time this week looking at myself. And my God, I'm gorgeous. Really, really sexy and pretty. In fact, one picture of me with no shirt on really nearly inspired me to take my pants off and pleasure myself, and it takes a lot to make me even think of partaking in an activity so gruesome, and that's just how beautiful this picture was - of me.

You see the thing is, after much research I found the girl I used to be in my past life! Her name is Françoise Dorléac and she was a French actress in the 1950s and 60s. She first performed on stage at the age of ten, and was a successful model as well as an actress, with a burgeoning career sadly cut short when she crashed her car and died at the age of twenty-five.

Everything about her fits nicely into the regressions I had in my past-life therapy session. She was famous from a young age, born into a theatrical family, with a famous actor for a father, and eventually a famous sister too, which would totally fit the kind of melancholy I felt about being loved as a celebrity but not as myself, and the feelings of 'having' to do things more than 'wanting' to do them. Especially being famous so young and being lusted after as a beautiful celebrity and therefore never being able to explore usual youthful relationships. Also, her star was on the rise, she had begun to work in English-speaking films, and was thought to be about to become a huge international star, which fits my feelings that I was seemingly getting pulled towards bigger and bigger fame, whether I wanted it or not.

She was engaged to a fellow actor but never married, which could quite easily fit my feelings that I was in a relationship set up by management rather than love. And as I saw in my therapy session, she crashed her car driving herself somewhere rural and not where she lived and worked, outside of Nice in France.

In the therapy session we also talked about a soul selecting their next life specifically to put right what was left unresolved in their past life, and she seems to fit this for me too. She was part of a family business, and possibly fell into it without ever really thinking about what she really wanted to do. Much like myself growing up around a family business, which I didn't finally decide was definitely not the life I wanted till I was 27. And I also have long felt a hole in my life for having missed out on the usual youthful innocent entry into romantic life (although for very different reasons). It is entirely possible that Françoise chose me as a way to re-live these experiences but this time to live long enough to conquer these issues, while simultaneously being able to become an artist on her own terms, not as a result of family expectation or driven by management.

Since my session I have looked into the lives of every actress ever killed in a car accident, and every other one had critical inconsistency in their story from what I saw in regression, everyone but Françoise Dorléac. If people do or can have past lives then this is one of the people I was. You should check out one of my movies one day, apparently I was excellent, and I was definitely beautiful. I mean, come on, what else are you going to do? Look at yourself looking at yourself? Don't do that, that's really creepy.

I'M FINALLY A TEENAGER

There comes a time in every young man's life that morphs him into a fully grown sexually aware man—you know, like those awesome guys you see at bars with all those hilarious lines? Here is one I came up with: 'have you ever wanted to throw used heroin needles at small children and then tried to vomit on a pigeon? Me neither, who knew we had so much in common!' Genius right? Use this and you typically discover that you have something in common with at least twenty percent of girls!

So you know what's coming right? Obviously I am about to talk about the time your Christian school tries to teach you about sex.

I wasn't the neophyte most sheltered 12 year olds are, oh no; I already knew a thing or two. One time a few months earlier I was reading a sex book I had found in a friend's dad's closet, and for some reason my penis got hard, and then when I rubbed it, hoping it would go soft again, instead something horrible happened - it had an epileptic fit!

The way it convulsed scared me so much I actually thought I was about to die. So being told by a schoolteacher about something called an 'orgasm' was welcome relief for a while, that is, until I heard about a type of person called a 'wanker', and that a wanker was about the lowest type of human you could be, and that I had unwittingly become one! Damnation.

Worse was to come, my relative calm about my sexual development was soon to go hardcore bye bye.

Our school, being an extremely expensive private school, passed the baton of teaching physical sexual development to science teachers, and as you may know, men who grow up with the right set of interests to inspire them to teach science to 12 year olds are freaking insane.

These are the people who love nothing more than conducting crazy experiments with all sorts of chemicals, playing with random animal organs, and in our teacher's case spreading urban legends like the one about the girl who tried to masturbate with a test tube until it exploded into a million pieces inside her vagina which had to be extracted one by one by a poor man with microscopic tweezers whose entire love of vagina was ruined by her bloody mess.

Our science teacher was also stone-cold addicted to talking about hermaphrodites. You know those guys who like heroin so much that they end up living on the streets and doing whatever they can to get one more shot of that stuff into their blood stream? Well, they're also addicts. It's a sad world sometimes.

If you don't know, a hermaphrodite is one of those delightful people who are born with indeterminate or sometimes both sexes' sexual organs. Sure, that is fascinating, I am not denying that at all, but this guy was a freaking addict. He talked about them constantly, he showed us videos of them, he led us in debates over certain cases and whether the doctors should have surgical changed them into all boy or all girl, and he even showed us a video of a doctor playing with a poor kid's newly handcrafted penis as he tried to enjoy his first erection.

Yet *most* horribly, and I mean life-alteringly terrifying, he also told us story after story of kids who did not show any signs of being any different to normal boys or girls until puberty hit and the boys would suddenly grow boobs and develop in other feminine ways, or the girls would suddenly grow dicks.

This....

PANICKED

Me.

I always knew I was different. I guess all kids probably feel this way, but because I had always been so small for my age for a boy,

I was able to utterly convince myself that I had found the answer to my affliction, because clearly, even though I had a penis, I was dead set pre-ordained to hit puberty and grow in a lovely set of breasts. After this, my hips would expand, as my curves came into shape, and then bizarrely the area under my scrotum would open up like a wound and a vagina would form, and I would eventually be a certified hermaphrodite.

I have long wished to be unique, but this was only like my seventh-most desired way to achieve this, and you better believe I was not yet ready to give up on the first six.

1. Be recognized as a supremely talented and original artist
2. Be given credit for world peace
3. Invent a new style of pants
4. Have a disease named after me
5. Get stuck up a tree while trying to rescue a celebrity's kitty
6. Get murdered in a public way by a notorious serial killer
7. Be a hermaphrodite

Also, I kind of want super hot famous women to start having sex with me, but you have to be realistic.

Once the seed was planted in my mind, I needed to know. I was *desperate* for puberty to hit. Grow into a normal boy and find sweet relief, or grow into a girl, play with my boobs till I got bored and then probably kill myself in shame. I didn't even really care which, I just required knowing.

I started to consume any porn I could get my hands near—I felt that if I overly sexually stimulated my mind I could trigger a wet dream—and as our awesome science teacher had told us, the wet dream was the place where puberty was born.

Sexualize my mind I did, but the wet dream did not come. Instead I developed a chronic issue with giving my penis epileptic fits. Even though I was still not showing even a hint of a sign of puberty, I epileptic fit myself so much my penis was often covered with open wounds from the constant chaffing (it's even worse when it's baby sized, because it's difficult to get a grip on).

With sex on my mind every minute of the day, but puberty staying away from me like a mouse living in a hole near a lion den, I developed yet another little quibble of delight. I decided that by 'wasting' all my hormones on my little habit, I was literally *causing* puberty not to happen. And yet I couldn't stop myself pleasuring myself, no matter how much I let myself self-loathe. It was a classic addiction—I didn't enjoy it, yet I couldn't stop, even though I knew it was harming me.

You can imagine my joy as puberty swept my peers while I remained a self-hating, dick-bleeding, pre-pubescent, masturbation addict convinced he was about to turn into a girl. Ahh, the joy of youth, the happiest time in any boy's life.

By the way, the teacher who inspired all this panic in me also once gave me a detention for messy handwriting. He couldn't read my notes on his obsessive hermaphrodite speeches and this made him mad. I hope your children also get the great education that horribly over-priced private schools can provide!

Puberty did come eventually, and I didn't grow boobs or a vagina. Also, my penis hasn't bled in years! Hoorah. I know puberty came because, in actual fact, no-joke seriousness – 22nd of July 2010 I finally had my first wet dream! Yes, at the age of 33! Sure, I still didn't get laid in this dream, I got close and then went and helped myself out, it's the closest I ever get to a sex dream, yet still I'm a man, baby, I'm a man. I kind of knew I would become a real man this year.

For some reason I feel like this should be celebrated in some way. My first thought was trying to score a threesome (I believe a dream skimming the surface of this may have inspired my new manhood), although I don't think this is going to happen anytime soon. In the meantime I think I might go back to imagining my body with boobs.

Update: Although I had mostly blocked this out I did in fact do something to celebrate my newfound manhood around the time of my first wet dream. I followed the well-beaten path of horny men doing something utterly ludicrous to try and get laid.

That's right, one night, after a few drinks, I decided to randomly text message a picture of my erect penis to a platonic, albeit extremely flirty, female friend.

Results:

1. No pictures of her vagina were sent in return
2. No offers for said erect penis to enter any part of her body were outlaid
3. If someone was to ask her if David Tieck has a penis with a side of vagina, she could comfortably and honestly say, 'I don't think so, and I've seen pictures.'

Also I eventually randomly saw that same girl recoil after touching a penis on an amateur porn site. The world is a strange place.

MIND GAMES

Given some of the stories I am telling in this book, it might surprise some of you to hear that I wasn't that happy as a teenager. In all reality, I was so miserable that I spent many long tear-filled hours contemplating suicide.

For a while I kept lots of knives around me—thanks, government, for allowing depressed teenagers to purchase huge knives at army-themed stores, we find so many ways to contribute to a vigorously healthy society with them.

I used them to contribute to society by night after night holding them over my heart trying to get the courage to plunge the knife in to sweet, horribly poorly thought-out, painful death. The mind of a suicidal teenager is a silly one. I spent so much time thinking about stupid and ultimately pointless crap that I never even thought about the fact that if I did get the guts to attempt to plunge in the knife, the chances of my weak little girl arms getting the blade through the chest cavity and anywhere near the heart were slim, and I'd just be in pain and have a horribly embarrassing wound to deal with. Also, my knife was nowhere near sharp enough to cause any damage because I'd used it to stab mattresses and pillows and all sorts of other things while imaging they were everyone from teachers, to kids I knew, to celebrities.

Fortunately, I never did attempt to plunge the knife in. I did attempt suicide eventually, though.

I was too scared to stab myself, cut my wrists, hang myself, jump off a cliff, or drink a bottle of Draino, and if my memory serves me correctly, I believe my biggest fear was making an unsuccessful attempt and having to face the embarrassment and ridicule that goes along with such things. So I had to come up with a method that no one would know about unless it worked.

Here is what I came up with—I decided to use my brain to talk my body into giving me cancer. Have I boasted about my high IQ in this book yet? Maybe I don't need to, sometimes it just speaks for itself.

Some people may think that trying to will my body into developing cancer was not a real suicide attempt, but believe me, it was. It wasn't just a fleeting thought one day, it was a long drawn-out arrangement of near meditation, where I would concentrate my thoughts on negatively manipulating my body's cells, morphing them into developing cancer. I did this a LOT! I did it in class at school, I did it walking around the shops, and I did it lying in bed in the dark *assuming* it would be successful.

Mind you, it wasn't a completely negative plan. Cancer, I figured, would not kill me instantly, it would be diagnosed and then I would have time. Time I planned to use wisely. I figured after being diagnosed with terminal cancer I could finally start to live. I could quit school. I could travel. And with my family feeling sorry for me they would surely buy me absolutely anything I wanted. And I could pay prostitutes to get naked in front of me. I surmised that six months or a year of doing anything I bloody wanted, with no fear for a future I no longer had to worry about, would be all I needed to die content. And dying was something I definitely wanted to do.

The real ludicrousness of this plan of course is that I genuinely thought my brain was powerful enough to intentionally induce cancer but it never even occurred to me to use it to induce happiness!

Cut to fifteen years after this stupid mental meltdown, and I had a weird lump growing on my left eyeball, right on the edge of the pupil. It wasn't big, but was kind of gross looking, often making my eye bloodshot, and it pulsated if I was out in bright sun. As a guy, I knew what I had to do; I raced to the doctor after only six months of worrying about it.

'It's basically like skin cancer,' the doctor said to me.

'Wait, what? I have skin cancer on my eyeball? No, no, no. What does this mean? Am I going to lose my eye and be a loser with an eye-patch or have some freaky glass ball I have to put in and take out? Or am I going to die? Oh my God. I never liked wearing sunglasses, ok. I found them uncomfortable, and sweaty when hot, and I have long eyelashes that rub against the lenses when I blink and it doesn't feel good! Still, does that mean it's all my fault? Fuck, fuck fuck, I don't want to lose my eye,' I thought as my mind raced in twelve directions over the next half a second.

'Only, it's not dangerous,' the doctor continued.

'Wait, what? Skin cancer, it's not dangerous?' I mumbled. 'WHAT KIND OF FUCKING PSYCHO OPENS WITH "IT'S LIKE SKIN CANCER" IF IT'S *NOT* DANGEROUS? I SHOULD KILL YOU, YOU FUCK!' I thought.

Turns out it's just like a growth on my eyeball, called a 'pterygium', and yes I may have to get it cut out one day, in what people have described as one of the most painful operations available to the human body, but for now I'm going to keep it. I don't really like scalpels near my eye, plus retarded nightclub bouncers often accuse me of being drunk because I have one bloodshot eyeball emanating from a lump on my eye, and I'd hate to give up that joy.

Still, if it had been a life-threatening form of eyeball cancer, I really would have had no one to blame but myself. Not just because I literally tried to give myself cancer, but also because I have kind of made fun of cancer a lot in my life, writing many jokes about it, like these:

- Shocking news: It's easier to remove prejudice from your heart with a knife than with a subscription to *Why Asians Deserve Cancer* magazine.
- Little known fact: The phrase 'here comes the unbelievably incentive cancer infected sock wearer' is not a popular phrase.

- How come you often hear of a bevy of beauties but only occasionally hear of a bevy of girls who breathe through throat-cancer neck holes? And
- Massive dick – good
  Massive stab wound – bad
  Massive raise – good
  Massive tumor – bad

Come on 'massive', make up your mind, are you good or bad? You're making the word cancer feel bad about itself, and frankly cancer has enough to worry about.

Clearly. I still think about stabbing too much, plus I have been flippant in my attitude toward cancer, and if cancer has a conscious mind, I have no doubt some of the time it's thinking, 'I'm going to kill that prick David Tieck.' The only thing I can do is kill it first. Fortunately, I do have a plan on how to cure cancer. Well, at least help with the process. Here is the pitch.

I believe two things, well many things, but also these specific two things:

1. The best way to avoid cancer is to live a healthy life
2. Most charitable cancer movements are really stupid.

It's all about wearing pink ribbons, or here in Australia growing a mustache, or buying daffodils, which are fine and dandy to raise some cash and awareness but do crap-all to actually reduce cancer rates. I want to start a cancer movement that simultaneously raises money AND reduces cancer rates by requiring healthier lifestyles. My movement will be an annual event where people set themselves some sort of health goal, from losing weight, to running a marathon, to quitting smoking. You announce to your friends and family what your goal is, and ask them to sponsor you, if you succeed in your goal their money goes to cancer research, and if you fail you have to pay up the money to research, giving you a super-sized motivation to get your ass to the gym and follow through. Money is raised, cancer rates reduced. Done. 'GENIUS' I may even say.

I decided to start my movement by volunteering to become a gym junkie for a couple of months and write a magazine article about it I'm calling 'Get Cut To Cut Cancer Rates' to raise awareness.

Consider this headline for the posters and television commercials: Are you willing to become way more attractive to cure cancer? Or would you rather be ugly and watch your loved ones die?

Done and done. Anyone who turns down that proposal is both too skinny and healthy and way to overwhelmed with sexy strangers to even notice the advertisements or else they are beauty-hating, cancer-loving scum. This is so good and valuable it can't possibly fail, right?

So I wrote out my pitch and sent it to magazines around the world, from *Esquire* to *Men's Health* and even *Cosmopolitan*.

So far my replies have amounted to zero. 'I'M TRYING TO CURE CANCER AND YOU CAN'T EVEN EMAIL ME BACK, YOU BEAUTY-HATING, CANCER-LOVING ASSHOLES!' Seriously! No one, *no one* wants to do this? FUCK ME.

Oh well, I tried to give myself cancer with my mind and now I have tried to use my mind to cure it. Seems balanced, right? I guess now I can go back to making fun of cancer, like these ways:

- I love girls with sun tans, I love knowing that they have such interesting and diverse interests that they choose to spend their free time literally lying doing nothing. I like rubbing my hands over skin not sure if I am touching a woman or if I am touching a Turkey that was overcooked then left out overnight and if I am really lucky I love getting to chew, like a chocolate chip in a ball of cookie dough, on a fresh mushrooming cancerous mole right off her shoulder.
- It turns out if your nickname is 'cancer face' and you have skin cancers on your face then your friends might be dicks!

Update: Not long after I sent my pitch out around the world, an organization started a familiar-sounding concept. The idea was to start a treadmill challenge, where people sponsored you to run on a treadmill and the more hours you did the more they would donate to cancer research. Only they messed up two things:

1. This only really does anything if your health problem is weight issues; why not take a wider scope, like my idea?
2. I was going to inspire change by taking an average pudgy bloke like myself and proving that he could change his ways and become healthier. These guys' concept was pitched by a model, a washed-up over-the-hill one married to one of the richest people in the world, you money-grubbing whore model, but a model nonetheless, those very people who inspire women to binge and purge and men to be so superficial that they can never settle for a real loving woman, and so instead get drunk every night hoping to beer goggle their way into any girl's pants. This is what you're advertising your 'health' pitch with?

Thanks a lot, you idiots, you've just taken us further away from a cancer cure and closer to emotional hell once more.

Update Two: There is now a TV show called *Dating in the Dark,* where they have men and women go on blind dates in the pitch black so they get to know each other's personalities without being swayed by looks. It proves that there is more to love than looks. And to prove a point the show is hosted by a smoking-hot model.

Can people please start listening to me rather than the morons so we can make some real positive changes to this world?

Update Three: I reckon if I actually did make the world a better place, I could get a totally hot girlfriend, maybe even a model!

Update four: I have now actually been a contestant on Dating in the Dark, man I am a hypocrite.

SUNSETS AND WALKS
ON THE BEACH

I was 19 years and 347 days old and I decided that if I hadn't at least held a girl's hand by the end of my teens then, you know, I'd hate myself even more than I currently did.

It was New Year's Eve and I decided for the first time I was actually going to go out and party or something similar to that. My friend and his girlfriend invited me to come along with some of her friends to see the fireworks and see what happened from there, and I decided this time I was going to have fun, and to see if I could talk a girl into one of those midnight kiss dealies for my first ever kiss.

We met up, and as usual I was not drinking but everyone else was, and I was having woeful awkward silence-riddled attempts at conversation with some of the girls in the group, and feeling horrible, when a change suddenly came over me. 'Stop being such a fucking loser,' I said to myself.

I decided for the second time in my life to drink alcohol. The girls had three beers they were going to throw in the trash because they were not allowed to take them on the train with them, so I downed the three of them in three big chugs, and got drunk quick.

Now it was *on!* I started hitting on some of the girls and within half an hour my two main targets were both making out with guys who just randomly said something to them walking past (one of these two girls would soon come out as a lesbian and find a girlfriend within days, which made me very jealous). I fell into my usual trap of self-pity at once again not being the one chosen, but then a miracle happened. 'Simone is going to come meet us,' my friend's girlfriend announced.

This was great news; I had wanted to meet Simone for a couple of weeks now. Why? Because I had been told two wonderful factoids about her; she was not considered attractive and she had recently attempted suicide. Why were these factoids wonderful? Because in my pea brain I thought, 'Holy shit, someone so depressed she wants to kill herself—she's someone even *I* could get!'

Yes, I was that radiatingly pathetic. I was actively chasing people who were literally trying to kill themselves.

Later that night, I had my first ever real conversation with a girl. Simone and I had absolutely nothing in common, but we were both so full of self-hatred that we somehow connected. And I found myself really, really liking her, or at least the idea that she was liking me, which was such a joyous feeling I couldn't help but like her back. I didn't get the guts to try and kiss her that night, but I did get enough information to get her phone number out of the book, and I did somehow get the guts to call her a few days later (from a pay phone in a remote area so there was no possibility of being overheard in case I did something horribly embarrassing).

We went on what may still be my only ever 'date', if you define a date as going out with the intent of getting to know someone better that you might kind of like, and after hanging out with her about ten more times doing not much I finally kissed her.

And it was immensely awful. 'My God, is this what I have craved for so long and it's this unpleasant? I really do no longer have a reason to live,' I thought, as I clumsily tried to lick her tonsils. That's right, I thought of suicide while kissing a girl for the first time, who was a girl I only had the confidence to chase because she was suicidal too. That's how awesome I am!

And yes, this momentous occasion took place a couple of days before my twentieth birthday, I think, or maybe a day or two past it—but you know, minor detail. The point is, of course I was a late starter, and unfortunately I haven't yet caught up quite as much as I would have liked.

Having said that, *The Drew Cary Show* was a nineties sitcom about a fat thirty-something man in Cleveland, Ohio who could never get ahead in life. One time while I was watching this show, I pressed pause, slid off my pants, and did something extremely natural and normal for a boy and is not something to be ashamed of at all, unless perhaps you're doing it while watching *The Drew Cary Show.*

It wasn't Drew, mind you, who got me all worked up, well not this time, anyway (those glasses were sexy and are super hipster cool now!); there was a girl who was playing his girlfriend for a while that I found immensely attractive and when I see a girl I like I don't hold back in my desire of sexual satisfaction, not this kid.

Cut to just recently, and my friend has invited me to a friend's farewell party. As I was car-less and prone to getting wildly drunk, a friend of my friend offered to come pick me up and holy diloly if this person didn't end up being this very same girl from *The Drew Carey Show*!

We got talking and it turned out we had enormous amounts in common (we both liked the arts and serial killers) and we became fast friends. One night after hanging out, she drove me home and before I jumped out of the car I kissed her right smack bang on the lips! Yep that's right, your wildest fantasies CAN come true! Also as far as I know she's NEVER contemplated suicide.

MY GUT IS MAGICAL

When I was a little kid my older brother convinced me that he had special powers. I don't remember all of the things he said these special skills could accomplish, but I do distinctly remember one time he magically made the crossing light turn green by simply playing with a toy airplane! It was astonishing; he played with the plane and then after a short wait the lights changed. Wow.

I am not sure what else he could do, I think he could use his mind to make people give him chocolate or something, but I know what his number one most undeniably powerful skill was—manipulating his brother David.

You see, my brother was wise enough to convince me that his particular powers did not arise through him being an alien or being bitten by a radioactive spider, but rather they were inside all Tieck boys, and if I was able to complete a number of tasks for him, he promised to share the powerful secrets with me so I too could be super.

These tasks included things such as putting things on my Christmas wish list, which I was then to give to him, and most notably the time he needed me to allow him to cover my entire head in sticky tape. I wanted these powers bad, so giving up a skateboard and a Space Invaders game were small sacrifices. The tape on the head, though? Well, that was going to cause a few issues.

I let him do it, of course. I just didn't know at the time just how painful it was going to be to try to pull it off again. Also, I forgot to take into account that I was a real little weakling (*David Tieck he is weak, David Tieck he is weak*—oh what marvelously imaginative and accurate bullies my peers were). So, after pulling out like two strands of tape I gave up and decided instead to be a pioneer of the arts.

This was the early eighties and punk rock was a music form I had never heard of, but I grabbed my mother's sharp sewing scissors, and hacked out all that sticky tape and most of my hair in huge chunks of sticking-it-to-the-man punk rock anarchy.

I went to school the next day looking like I had been in a fight with a hair-eating condor, and in an act of youthful revolt said, 'My mum cuts my hair and she isn't any good at it.' Social services were probably called, and I looked like a freak for a few weeks before my hair grew back enough to even it out, and for some reason my brother never really talked about those powers again.

That is, except for years later when he started to say that *I* had powers. Psychic powers! I predicted things for him too often to consider them coincidence. They were usually tiny things, like predicting what was about to happen in sporting events, but it was enough for him to at least believe it was possible.

And he was right!

I am goddamn psychic, sometimes in life-changing ways.

When I was about ten years old, every day when I walked home from school there was a major highway I had to cross. At this time in the afternoon the traffic was heavy on the far side of the road and almost non-existent on the near side, so every day I would cross halfway and stand on the median strip waiting for the light to go green. One particular day, for some unknown reason, I decided not to walk halfway; it wasn't that I felt like being patient or lazy, it was an instinct that specifically told me not to. Moments later a car got clipped by another car going at high speed and the car lost control and slammed hard into the pole where I would have been standing on any other day. It would have been impossible for me to survive. Then about six or seven years ago I was at the local mall, having just been to a doctor's appointment. This particular appointment was for me to receive results of a biopsy and after a horrible two weeks of waiting I had just found out I didn't have cancer. I was heading to the mall for a part celebratory and part consoling dessert of some description, when I had to cross a street. It was usually a pretty quiet street, despite being in a busy area, and by the time the light turned green for me to cross, the rest of the pedestrians had crossed against the red, something I rarely do, and especially here, as there was a blind corner where you could only a see a car coming really late. I have seen people nearly hit there dozens of times and I have since learned several pedestrians have been killed there recently. So I waited for the green and got ready to cross. On this particular day, however, with my head in the clouds with the joy of not having cancer and yet with the doctors still not sure what the hell was causing my never-ending ear infection, just sure it was 'something', in their words, I waited for the green, but instead of crossing when the little green man showed himself, something told me to step back, so I did. In that moment a car coming around the blind corner realized he hadn't made the orange light but was in no position to stop for the red and to compensate for his error and try to get through the intersection as fast as humanly possible he instead sped up and took the corner as close as he possibly could, meaning he clipped the gutter and missed me by less than an inch. Once again, if not for a strange instinct I would surely have been killed. I don't know what this instinct was either of these times, but it saved my life. I don't think I regularly have instincts that turn out to be nothing. I do have the kind of abnormal mind that I can't look at a speeding car without constantly visualizing it crashing, I can't see a pedestrian sprinting in front of a speeding car without imagining them being hit. I visualize all the possibilities in most of the situations I am in. Still, on these two occasions I didn't just see the possibilities and react just in case, instead I had a gut feeling that I listened to, and it saved my life.

More recently I have wanted to explore this aspect of my life so I have been reading a book on how to look for gut psychic feelings proactively rather than just wait for them to come on their own. One weekend, on a Saturday night, I was crashing at a friend's place for a while in a part of town I did not know at all, on the fringe of

Korea Town in Los Angeles. I was all alone, desiring a fun night and so spontaneously while out walking I decided to proactively ask my gut to lead the way, and do everything it told me to do.

The first thing my gut told me was that a good night for me meant it needed to guide me towards a meaningful connection with another human being (get me laid) or lead me to a unique and enriching experience of some sort (get me laid). Was my gut up for the job? I was willing to give it a shot.

My gut distinctively pointed me north, right into Korea Town, and strongly warned me away from several bars and clubs I walked past.

What I did, at every corner or establishment, was imagine the options and see what it felt like in my gut while considering each option, and it quite clearly had different opinions, and gave different responses, even at times in direct contrast to my conscious thoughts.

For example, it suggested I head down a street I had never been down, and believed to be headed back to suburbia and away from the nightlife my conscious mind was looking for. But I followed, and it sent me down another street, where I found what looked to be a huge bar and club that I had no idea was there.

My gut told me that I should go in, yet not right away, and instead sent me on a mission to buy and drink a Red Bull, but then it clearly wanted me to go back there. I showed my ID, and was sent up a stairwell, and as I ascended the stairs I got the noticeable sense that although I was supposed to proceed, something was not right about this.

As I reached the top, the smell of sterilization was very strong, and I found a tiny little bar adjacent to a quiet hallway that had numerous doors to what looked like bedroom-sized rooms. My gut knew its mission was to get me laid and had led me to a freaking brothel! Hey, if my psychic powers are telling me to have sex with a prostitute, I am supposed to, right?

Only, it wasn't a brothel. All the little rooms were not bedrooms but small karaoke booths for private parties. This was super weird. I went for a wander and found almost all the rooms to be empty, and they looked like offices set up for conference rooms, not places to party. The full ones were like sadness holes where six friends sang songs together in a super claustrophobic antisocial way. I had no idea places like this existed, and I still have no idea *why* they exist, but my gut told me to hang, to sit and drink one beer in a room all alone, then quickly told me to get the hell out of there (update: I now LOVE these Karaoke rooms!)

For a moment I got mad at my gut, calling it a moron, but it shot back that it was specifically trying to delay me for some reason. I had promised I would listen to it tonight, and so my faith returned. And over the next couple of hours my gut seemed to tell me quite loudly that it was fighting a tight time schedule, speeding me up and slowing me down in a carefully monitored balancing act. I felt it wanted me somewhere specifically at a specific time, but it just had to work out how to make that happen bit by bit.

He kept sending me north, although one time he took me around the block specifically so I could watch a really drunk guy try and fail miserably to ride a bike. That was kind of funny.

Dewy, as my gut now named himself, instinctively guided me towards a German beer hall with a traditional Korean menu. Dewy asked me to order a couple of beers and take out my pad and write, and listening to his advice, I randomly wrote this.

> "If you ask me, most marksmen are probably *really* bad at remembering to pay for their parking at the machine before driving up to the exits and annoying the people behind them, the very people who HAD taken the time to follow the clearly labeled directions as posted in several different hard-to-miss locations upon entering the parking facility. I know—I am making a bold statement here, and if you know me, I don't like making bold statements: bold type uses more ink when printing and that shit is surprisingly expensive. Then again, I was the guy who once boldly claimed that one day people would suddenly realize that:
>
> 'Hey, cheese is awesome, and therefore using the term "cheesy" translated to mean something other than awesome,

or maybe even dare I say it "uncool" (how can something be un something, really you're either something or you're not it, you're not un it. I am a boy not an ungirl, for example. Or I didn't cut down a baby giant redwood today I didn't unnotcutdownababygiantredwood today because that would be kind of stupid, giant red woods are awesome, so you can stick your uns up your ass. By the way, if you choose not to do this, then please don't unstickunsupyourass). So "cheesy" should be awesome, always, unless you're being ironic and, let's face it, when people use the word "cheesy" they're hardly ever meaning it ironically and frankly if you're going to be ironic leave cheese fucking out of it, cheese is never ironic to you, it's just delicious, and it sits on top of awesome foods like pizza or inside awesome foods like pizza with cheese stuffed into the insides, so leave cheese alone is all I am saying.'

And yes, that is a direct quote of what I thought ALL people would one day randomly say out loud. It was a bold statement and I only turned out to be partly true (the true bit was the word 'something'—that word actually exists!)

By the way, feel free to be ironic about mirrors—you look at *them* but you see *yourself*! Wow, there has got to be something ironic about that.

Hey check this out—what did the vain guy say to the mirror?

Nothing!

Get it? He didn't see the mirror, only himself, ha ha, you know, 'cause he was vain and vanity is awesome.

By the way, if you're vain, you suck, so I am so glad I am so much more awesome and beautiful than you, it makes me feel awesome about myself, you vain bastard.

I feel like we've gotten off the point. What point, I hear you ask? (Wow, either you're really loud or we live closer than I thought!) Point is, you can see why I would be wary about making a bold statement again, that is why when I say marksmen probably show an arrogant level of diligence and assiduousness (thesaurus = yay), when it comes to parking etiquette you can have faith I wouldn't be making such a claim if I didn't have some hardcore evidence that I know what the hell I am talking about.

What hardcore evidence do you have, I hear you ask (seriously, keep it down. 'The neighbors will talk' is a phrase which suggests neighbors are mostly mute and I think evidence points towards *most* neighbors NOT being mute—so just be careful is all I'm saying).

So what evidence do I have? The best kind, that's what, yes, that's right. Hell yeah, I have myself in the possession of a theory!

Do you know that it was a theory that led to the invention of tablecloths? Someone once said, 'I have a theory that if we cover the table with a cloth we can create more laundry with no real benefits at all', and an international billion-dollar industry was born. So there is proof that theories can change the world! When was the last time photographic evidence changed the world? It's probably been a week or so, where as tablecloths are fresh and relevant.

And really, if you can't get mad at an entire profession because of a theory, then what is the point of those public service announcements about how it's probably not ok to light your own arm on fire? I know! *They* DON'T exist, because someone had a theory that if they did make public service announcements of this variety it would be pointless because the type of individual prone to lighting their arms on fire are probably too busy with active dating lives to be at home watching TV.

And they were of course right—yet another reason I am jealous of the fire-armers. The other reasons include the following:

- They rarely have their sinks blocked up with hair that has fallen off their arms, which saves thousands a year in plumbing costs

- They're more respected that politicians
- They rarely get given tickets by the cops (when your arm is on fire the cops *believe* you when you say your wife is about to give birth, 'cause think about it: if your wife wasn't about to give birth, why on earth would you light your arm on fire?)

By the way, remember high school when all your classmates' wives were giving birth? If so, your peers had a weird trend of young marriages.

I once wrote a novel called *Your Peers Had A Weird Trend Of Young Marriages*. It was about a bunch of normal, well-adjusted teenagers—the title was ironic—and yes, it's way better to be ironic about peers and teenage marriages than cheese, you dairy-hating scum. (Butter and ice cream are also dairy! Wow, magical. Have you ever put melted butter on your ice cream? If so, you may be overweight, and yet clearly awesomenessous, which is proof that fat is the new cool).

Speaking of scum, I also assume marksmen are dairy haters, because why else would they not pay for their parking at the time they were told to! I'll tell you why—marksmen don't know the meaning of the word 'helmatumliciss' because that word doesn't exist and marksmen are often too busy looking into that close-up scope eye-hole dealy to worry about the dictionary. Yes, I know—bastards.

And what kind of person doesn't have intimate knowledge of every made-up word not in the dictionary? People who don't pay for their parking when they should, that's who! (Please note: Also, *all* people, and *all* people *includes* marksmen!)

So yes, do I answer yes to the suggestion that yes I am pissed off at marksmen? Yes I do.

Will I get over it soon? Probably, I mean, I don't actually know any marksmen and I don't own a car, so I rarely park one in car parks, so what's the big deal really?

By the way marksmen are those guys who train to like shoot things from far away right? 'Cause those guys are talented AND cool; I'd never say anything bad about them.

PS—helmatumliciss: To love tablecloths and yet keep it a secret that really they don't do anything but contribute to laundry.

Thanks for that, Dewy. You clearly felt that this needed to be said to the world, and made sure I had the perfect quiet bar to work on it.

Dewy now sent me to a weird sports bar where Koreans ate American bar food like chicken wings and mozzarella sticks with chopsticks and ignored the football on TV.

Dewy told me to drink one more beer then he said he wanted me specifically on Melrose Avenue. I ordered a different brand of beer than the one I had just consumed and this one came lumpy, yes lumpy, and no I do not want to speculate on what made it lumpy, only that I *don't* waste beer, so I still drank it, but quickly, as if Dewy clearly wanted me to leave quicker than a non-lumpy beer would have taken me.

As I was walking up Western Ave, Dewy was clear: get to Melrose, which was a few blocks north. As I got close, I got a phone call. It was from a friend of mine who I have a very flirty relationship with, and she had just been on an awful Internet date and wanted to see what I was up to.

'Walking up Western, closing in on Melrose,' I told her.

'Oh my God, I am at a gas station at the corner of Melrose and Western putting air in my tires as we speak!' she replied.

I went and met her and we spent a couple of lovely hours together. I was asked to stay at her place and do naughty things to her, but Dewy told me not to, and I listened, and was thankful I did after I went home, had a super rejuvenating fourteen hour sleep, and woke up knowing I would have regretted it had I stayed over. I am leaving America in two weeks; why I am not sure, I just feel like it's the right time, and I am out of cash. And given this fact I don't need to complicate friendships by sleeping with friends while they were bad-date vulnerable and I was lumpy beer tipsy and being psychic. Although, that is a super awesomenessous pick up line: 'Hey baby, I'm a little lumpy beer tipsy and there is a dude in my gut named Dewy and he totally thinks I should bone you tonight!'

So, I am still not sure about Dewy. Did my gut really manipulate my entire evening to make it so I was flukishly a block from a friend right at the moment she was calling me looking for a friend to hang out with? Or was it just a load of coincidental bollocks?

I have no idea, but Dewy says 'I got you into a cute girl's apartment *and* once again you were *not* hit by a car, so show me some respect, you ungrateful bastard.'

AND NOW PREDICTIONS FOR HOW THE WORLD WILL BE IN THE YEAR 2072 AND 255 DAYS By PSYCHIC DAVE:

- People no longer run off to join the circus, now the circus comes home with its tail between its legs in hope of joining you
- A new music trend called 'shunderling' has swept the world. Parents don't get it and Kanye West still hasn't made any unique or interesting music
- There are no longer months, as the political correct movement first renamed them 'differently calendarlyabled', and then eradicated them as being altogether separatist in nature; basically the point is that the politically correct movement is still totally retarded
- People have finally tuned into how birds really eat. Now when we feed ducks we vomit in their mouths
- Sex robots came and went, but sex milkshakes took off big time. People are now fat and satisfied
- People no longer rake leaves after it was discovered you can train dogs to eat them, now people just rake leafy dog poo

- Skydiving and squashing bugs have been combined into a hugely popular yet very bloody sport
- The fashion trend to wear clothes quite wrinkled has come and if this one ends there's going to be murder sprees
- There are no longer people we consider to be fat, because we're all fat; there are fewer people injured from sex though
- People have gotten realistic; we now have dessert first then ask if anyone has room for salad
- The town drunk is once again an admired member of society; unfortunately there's a really long waiting list for the position
- Carrots have finally taken the lead in their 30-year battle to be the most chipped vegetable
- A man celebrated being the ultimate winner at a cockroach-eating contest when he quit before starting
- There's now a third number to consider when you're going to the toilet. Number 3—when you diarrhoea out your bellybutton
- Frogs stage an unsuccessful revolution inspired by frustration over human drinks hogging all the tiny umbrellas
- Curtains have been renamed 'cruelty to Peeping Tom sheets' and we're all much happier because of it

It's going to be one hell of a few decades and 255 days—hope you're looking forward to it!

NONE OF YOUR BUSINESS

In the past year and a half of living on and off in Hollywood, seeing celebrities has become just a usual part of my life, and yet just infrequent enough that it's still kind of cool when it happens. Actually, more than that, it makes me smile with glee and call up all my friends and say, 'Guess who I saw?'

Consider these three true stories:
1. I once chatted to Ginnifer Goodwin from, among other things, *Big Love, Ed* and *Walk the Line*, at adjacent movie ticket machines and she is a girl I've long had a crush on and I actively wished she wanted my penis.
2. I once chatted to Kevin Connolly, from *Entourage*, while using adjacent urinals while I was holding my penis.
3. I once ran into Gwyneth Paltrow waiting for her limo in front of my building and my penis was completely unaffected.

That's right, not only do I frequently spend time with celebrities, but also two out of three times my penis comes into play!

I am a bit of a celeb whore. I like to claim, as a writer, it's my duty to stay up to date with pop culture. I like to say, as an artist, I am drawn to other artists. Both are true, yet total bullshit. I want to be on the inside, man; I want to date them, be friends with them and work with them. I think in my case it's an offshoot of being an outcast most my life and knowing that celebrity inner sanctum is the opposite. It's incast so much that there are endless magazines, TV shows, blogs and good ol' fashioned conversations over warm beverages about it. It'd be the ultimate revenge of the shy guy, who couldn't talk but is now talked about, and in an envious way.

I would like to make fun of myself here for how ridiculous this really is, especially since I even get excited when I see a celebrity I don't like, but I also kind of get excited when a plane crashes and lots of people die. It's not that I am a celebrity worshiper or an enormous psycho who gets pleasure from misery, I just like having something interesting to tell people.

'Did you hear what happened in France?'

'No, what?'

'Plane crash, two hundred dead.'

'Holy shit, that's horrible!'

'I know.' (And I got to be the one to tell you, yippppeeeee!)

'Any celebrities die?' (This would be me asking this now, as I get special pleasure from celebrities dying. (Ok, I admit it, I am psycho, or maybe it's just because I spent so long never having something to say that finally having something I *know* people will find interesting excites me. Well ok, both.)

These days, the most likely celebrities to die should be the so-called young starlets, who go batshit crazy on drugs and then frustratingly get clean just before dying. It's like a shitty movie with no ending. Boo. You know who you are, starlets, you've been to rehab, you've had DUIs, you've had sex tapes, and spent eight minutes in jail. Ok, that's the body of the story, now it ends with you in a grave, ok, so HURRY UP AND DIE! (Ok, just psycho.)

I was trying to think of a challenge I could set myself to overcome this desire for celebrity gossip. I figured maybe I needed to see lots of them, and see them at their worst to get to the reality of the sadness of the story. And various people have told me that the best place to see celebrities in Hollywood may just be Alcoholics Anonymous, where A-listers stand beside street junkies as equals in addiction.

With an interesting celebrity sighting in mind, I decided to check out a real Hollywood AA meeting.

I did some research on where all the AA meetings are, and tried to figure out where the best celebrity-spotting ones would be, when something hit me—I am not an alcoholic, and going to one of these meetings just to gawk at people at their lowest moments is really, really wrong!

What the hell is wrong with you, Dave?

But then again, well...um, I kind of *DO* drink way too much.

It basically started around two years ago. I'd been briefly dating a girl whom I'd long had a crush on, and was liking her and our potential future very, very much, when she abruptly ended it, and immediately started seeing someone else she clearly had hooked up with before we broke up, and someone she seemed to like way more than me, right away. Although this has been the common theme in my relationships, this one had been going amazingly well and I was not expecting it at all, and was not even barely ready to deal with it.

I literally didn't sleep for ten days. I had some half-sleep stuff on the couch in front of the TV, but I rolled around all night, and wallowed, oh my God did I wallow, and it just got worse and worse the longer I didn't sleep. On day eleven I was in so much body-twitching insomnia pain that I decided to drown it, and drank the best part of a bottle of vodka to inspire a beautiful nightmare-filled twenty hours or so of sleep.

Realizing that the past ten days had been about as much hell as I was ever going to experience unless I ended up in a prisoner of war camp, I decided for the next twenty nights or so in a row I would not just repeat this pattern, but spur on the misery and escalate it as much as possible! Why? For my art!

I'd spend a couple of hours every night drinking beer, and during this phase of the evening I would use my every brain cell I wasn't murdering welling up as much emotion as I could, going over and over all my worst memories, picturing my new ex (who I never slept with, by the way) making love to this new guy in every way imaginable while whispering in his ear, 'I'm so glad I found you, the last guy I dated was such a tool.' I'd think of unending loneliness. I'd think of getting diseases that would make me lose limbs, and grow huge warts all over my face and having to confront the public like that. I dreamed of being dumped, and cheated on, and used, and laughed at, and ridiculed. I thought of every bad thing happening to me that could imagine, for a couple of hours, while getting drunk alone, and getting myself into a state that had me shaking with sadness.

Then I'd write.

I ended up writing the most love-hating novel I imagine has ever been written. It opens with a four-year-old murdering his two-year-old brother, and the misery just flows from there. This novel is full of incest, rape, sexual abuse of children, war, murder, pain and hate, all told by people who are totally justifying their actions in ways, I hope, people will totally be able to understand and forgive. I think it's kind of brilliant, and probably either nowhere near as bad as I think (given that my memory of it is tainted by the state I wrote it in) or is every bit that radiantly awful that it is unpalatable and unpublishable. Regardless, I am glad I wrote it. (It's called *Comfortably Paranoid* and will be available as an e-book soon).

Still, as I did, I crossed a line that I had been trying to avoid for a long time. As a life-long horrible insomniac, I have very often been tempted to have a bunch of drinks exclusively to help me sleep, but never succumbed to temptation. But I had now drunk not for fun, but to tap into a different part of my creative brain, and to cure insomnia.

Having stepped over that line, this was to become a 'cure' I would turn to more and more. The more I did drink to sleep meant the harder and harder getting to sleep became when I didn't drink to sleep. Soon it was just about the only way I could sleep. I tried other remedies I promised I never would, like Nyquil, and over-the-counter sleeping pills, but they never worked and so I returned too often to drinking, drinking, and more drinking.

And here came the classic signs of alcoholism: drinking alone, hiding drinks around the house and experiencing blackouts!

But I refused to quit. Not because it wasn't bad for me—it was clearly horrible for me—but because this was a short-term problem that I could fix with a change of habits, and a little self-control. By which I mean time for a plan, dedicate myself to no more drinky drink for the wrong reasons. Simple. Screw you, AA. I refuse to believe that excessive drinking means you must never drink again. Drink when it's fun, don't drink when it's not, or is clearly stupid. It's not like I am fighting a twelve-year heroin binge here, I'm just an insomniac who likes to party and forgot not to blur the lines. First step admit you have a problem. Second step attempt to fix it.

Ok, let's do this. Mental decision made—check. Here is how it panned out for the first week.

Day 1: two beers at dinner with a friend, but no binging later—check. No drinking at bedtime—check. So, how did my first night of being healthy go? Well, at 2:49am I was eating peanut butter with a spoon. Hmm, not a good start.

But then a miracle happened, I fell asleep and I dreamed that a bunch of misfit Hollywood starlets had upped their crazy antics by staging public live sex shows in malls, as discovered, filmed and reported on by the cast of *Seinfeld*, and I lost my long waited-for front row seat when a cute girl camping out in front of me asked me to go get her coffee but I didn't know how to make coffee (I really don't) and I made a huge mess by converting coffee into gallons of undiluted water and dirt, which I spilled everywhere, which I tried to clean up, and then went in a futile search for a toilet 'cause I was busting.

I also had a dream about a son born from my sperm, who was a ferret, with super powers, and how all the other animals were trying to take him down, you know, once he got caught breaking animal flying regulations, and my efforts to protect him, before I went in a futile search for a toilet, 'cause I was busting.

When I woke up, surprisingly, I found I was busting to go to the toilet. As I urinated, I was forlorn; I guess alcohol-free sleep meant my dreams were going to be way more based in reality than the even more bat-shit crazy I am used to, sigh. At least I did sleep, though.

Day 2: I had a couple of free drinks as provided at a networking mixer I attended, but again I didn't go on with it, and wow I slept deep and long. Mental decision to sleep is freaking working.

This time I dreamed I had voluntarily joined a cult only to catch the leader out on a lie, but couldn't talk my fellow culters into leaving with me. I was a popular member of the cult so they still let me hang around, and I continued to do my homework, as I hate being a bad student, even in a cult, but over time my impassioned speeches encouraging my friends to leave, and the one time I forgot to double check what I had written for an old assignment before going up to read it in front of everyone and discovered it was just a big list of girls in the cult I had crushes on, and some thoughts I had as to how I would like to manifest this, led to me being relegated to the fringe of the social side of the cult. So I stopped at the cult convenience and bookstore and was appalled at how much the orange juice cost, and decided once and for all to quit. It was sad really.

Sleep man, sleep! This is good.

See how easy it is to repair things in your life, just by making decisions (says the guy who thinks it's impressive to go two days without binge drinking)? Also, if you love to learn about World War II you get called a WWII buff, so if you love to get buff, why aren't you called a 'buff buff'? Is it because that's a silly name and those guys are more pathetic than silly?

Day 3: I got to sleep...eventually. I dreamed I took a job in a bar that taught beer appreciation like a university course. Hmm, I wonder what my mind is missing?

Day 4: Mostly uneventful. I think this is a good sign.

Day 5: I went to Hooters, and for some reason there were mostly guys in there, they should really look at their menu and see what about it isn't female friendly! I was baffled, so I had a couple of beers and woke up feeling like someone was smashing metal with sledgehammers right next door! Fortunately, of course, I had only had a couple of beers, and I don't get hangovers—someone really *was* smashing metal with hammers next door! I'm no builder, but they were laying hardwood floors next door and I am POSITIVE that doesn't require four hours of sledgehammering metal!

Day 6: I woke up feeling intense optimism and with a gut feeling that as soon as I get back to Australia (which is soon) things are going to really take off for me. I had a lazyish day, ate some bad food at a Mexican place, watched a four year old ask for more chips and who then got told if he was still hungry he had to have breast milk, and tried not to watch as she breast fed him at the table, while her teenage daughters watched, and then I got some work done while dealing with construction next door.

Then it was Friday night, exactly one week before my final departure from Los Angeles. I had been staying with a friend in Long Beach, south of LA, for a couple of days while we were working, but I was very keen to spend my last weekend partying in Hollywood, and seeing some improv shows. Yet, I couldn't get there. With no car the only way I could figure out to get back to Hollywood involved buses through Compton, and from my memory of *Boyz in the Hood* and NWA's 'Straight out of Compton', this was a bad idea. You see, all the young men there are so darling you can't help but want to give them all gold stars for being excellent to one another, and I didn't have any gold stars! It's a tragedy that sometimes sees the National Guard and riot squads called in to hand out the stars themselves, but I couldn't bring myself to risk seeing the disappointing looks on these boys' faces when they were randomly nice to other kids just because of how much they liked each others' contrasting bandana colors, only to discover they were not rewarded with gold stars. Frankly, I think if the gold stars don't start flowing more freely, dare I say it, someone might one day do something mean to someone in Compton. Boo.

We went to the Outback Steak House for dinner, just for the irony, although I found myself surprisingly proud of the Australiana and the fact that we are liked enough to inspire a huge nationwide chain.

Boobs – Hooters
Rock n' Roll – Hard Rock Café
Australia – Outback Steak House

Three things I love and they all have restaurants, awww. While I was in the bathroom, 'Goodbye Hollywood' was being sung by Billy Joel. Nostalgia, bless my tearing-up eyes.

My friend Faith was supposed to come pick me up to take me back to Hollywood, but she was still working and running late. So my other friend, Bec, and I decided to go to the Long Beach Laugh Factory to catch the end of their show, and even though we had missed most of the show already, they told us we still needed to pay full price and still had to adhere to the two-drink minimum. Boo. (A few months later I went to the Hollywood Laugh Factory and after seeing one excellent show I tried to buy tickets to the later show, but while waiting where I was told by a staff member to wait for stand-by tickets. The house manager came up to me and yelled, 'You were at the last show, weren't you? You can't just hang out here all night, get the hell out!' 'No wait,' I protested 'I am trying to get a stand b...' but before I could finish, he said, 'I don't care, I want you out of this building right fucking now.'

For the record, Laugh Factory, if you ever burn down and several of your staff burn to death, I'll be the one adhering to the first half of your name. Actually, that's too harsh—just fire that fucking cunt (if you could have seen his facial expressions, body language and tone of his voice, you'd totally understand. I have never been written off as scum by another person anything like this ever, and I'm the guy who lived the rest of the stories in this book!) right now, let me pour lighter fluid on his face, take a match to it, then let me piss the fire out and all is forgiven.

Instead, we wandered into an Irish Bar to have a couple of lazy drinks. Once inside, I realized I loved this bar immensely. It had a great vibe, all sorts of people, and everyone was friendly, having fun and in good spirits. I had obviously decided I didn't want to over-drink tonight, but a guy offered to buy me an Irish Car Bomb, just cause he wanted someone to drink one with, so who was I to refuse? Faith let me know that she was supposed to go horseback riding at 9am the next day and asked me if I minded if we didn't head back to Hollywood tonight. Two hours earlier I may have, but now I was in super good spirits, having fun and in no rush to leave.

The band was playing songs we used to sing in school assemblies re-configured into Irish drinking songs. The crowd was having a good time to a man. This is what bars are supposed to be like. I started to dance a bit and frankly I was feeling about as good as I ever did, full of happiness, start-of-the-buzz fun phase of drinking, optimistic for the future, and happy to be around the people I was with.

I went for a bathroom break and on the way there I spotted a cute blonde. She was just my type; cute, petite, and adorable. I smiled at her and when I gave her the look back over my shoulder, she was doing the same. Holy shit, that NEVER happens! Yay!

On my way back I simply said, 'Want to come dance?'

Twenty minutes later she was sucking my tongue so hard that she actually tore the bit below on that floppy bit where the tongue connects to the mouth.

Wait, wait—back up a moment. It turned out it was her twenty-fifth birthday, although, like me, she looked young for her age. We got on like old friends from the get go. She was sweet, and even got endearingly mad at me when I kissed her with my eyes open. This was the type of girl who, if she worked at a certain comedy club would actually be fired for a complete inability to be a cunt, something that is required of staff at their venues. I was completely smitten.

I have had drunk make-out sessions a bunch of times in my life. This one was different; there was a bond. There was 'lavid'. There was a connection on numerous levels.

Just in case you were hoping, or just wondering, this is not one of those books that ends with me finding the 'one'. Yet so many things could have, and should have meant we were not in the same place at that specific time. The millions of 'ifs' that alter every moment of our existence, that at the time had me at unable to at least wonder and hope that fate was real.

The morning after this night, she was on my mind, and my phone was out of credit, and the Internet was down so I couldn't contact her, but as besotted as I was, I was clear enough of mind to write the following:

I am going home in six days, and she lives in Orange County, Los Angeles. The chances of us ending up together are slim. The point is this—for the first time in a long, long time I have made a connection with a girl that has me thinking those crazy thoughts like 'maybe I can get her to move to Australia with me' or maybe fate will send her a job offer to Sydney, or send me a job offer back to LA. I don't know what is going to happen, but I like it. I like the fantasy, and I like that my jaded attitude to romantic relationships is back to a phase where I can once again image meeting the right girl and having something meaningful. Two days ago, I didn't think I would ever feel that again.

We did see each other again. We went bowling, had a couple of beers, shared a hot tub, and I somehow read our awkward conversation as her telling me she'd had enough of me and wanted me to go home, when she told me later that apparently she meant the opposite. Stupid Dave! STUUUUUPID!

So now I'm going out for a beer, then another beer before I head back to Australia, but I will keep the drinking under control (at least the drinking alone to sleep part, I still plan to party baby, where else am I going to have my tongue torn by the sucking of hot blondes?). I know I will adhere to this, because for one I am sick of it, and secondly I plan to be a celebrity one day and I'd hate some loser to be running around enjoying telling people, 'Did you hear, David Tieck died, choked on his own vomit, and I GOT TO TELL YOU!'

DON'T READ THIS CHAPTER
IF YOU'RE OFFENDED
BY THE C WORD

Life is full of ups and downs, ins and outs, fun times and horrible times, sweet people and of course cunts. Plus, my God, moving house and country sucks. It's time consuming, tedious, hard, frustrating work and it forces you to take stock of all the stuff you own that you don't use but could use the money you spent on it.

As I packed up my last year and a half of living in the United States, hating wasting time putting stuff in boxes when I have an awesome city to see for the last time in a long time, feeling melancholy and dejected, yet excited about the next phase of my life, I could not help but think about a worse thing than moving. Actually far, far worse is watching your very recently ex-girlfriend move out of this very same apartment to move in with the guy she replaced you with.

The following is a piece I wrote a day or two after this happened to me earlier this year. The parts in the italics are my after-the-fact commentary of my state of mind back then. For some reason I decided to title this piece: Bouncy bounce!

It turns out that watching your ex, the most significant relationship of your life, move out of the home you had built together actually kind of sucks balls. *Wow, I started off understating things, this will not continue.*

The irony of course is the fact that this is the very person who once joyfully and literally sucked your balls in this very home doesn't improve the deal one little bit. *Actually, I am pretty sure she never sucked my balls, plus I have never enjoyed having that done, don't understand how anyone ever would, and frankly despite being the best and longest relationship of my life we barely even had sex after a couple of cunts smashed their cars into hers and left her with such severe back pain that I was left with blue balls. The whiny bits are supposed to be restricted to the original piece, but my god the fucked-up luck I've had when it comes to getting fucked, is just a total cunt!*

By the way, the reason this happened is because while I had recently been stuck out of America with visa problems keeping me from my love, another guy decided to take the opportunity to move in on her and in her and all the other things I really don't want to think about, DESPITE knowing she already had a boyfriend, I know! *By 'I know' I am assuming you all consider this as despicable as I do, but I know many of you don't. This makes me sad.*

Now, I don't know this guy at all, but I do know beyond a shadow of a doubt that this is a cunt act. In fact, this is the type of cunt act that is performed exclusively by cunts, and only by cunts and therefore this cunt act has in fact provided definitive proof that this guy is in fact a cunt. *In hindsight, I don't take this back at all.* And I most certainly hope that one day he catches a rare disease which makes his penis bleed painfully every day for weeks in a very 'did someone stab me in the penis hole with a wide-bladed knife and I just kind of didn't notice somehow' way. Then I would like his penis to abruptly explode one day while he is in a busy place, with such a force that rapidly separating penis flesh would burst through the front of his pants, leaving him to bleed to death while lying on the floor and crying over and over again, 'My penis is gone, my penis is gone.' Because cunts should die with a bleeding hole between their legs, that's called irony. *Oh I get it, because 'cunt' is another word for 'vagina', and those are sometimes bleeding holes. Nice use of irony, Dave, I love it!*

And if anyone wants to point out to me that the REAL irony is of course that while I was writing this fantasy he and my ex were probably celebrating officially moving in together and she was showing her joy by sucking his balls then I shall stab you in the face (by far my favorite place to imagine stabbing someone). *Wow, thanks Dave, you just made me visualize them doing it again, you were supposed to be getting mad at him, not forcing yourself back into that pit of despair!*

Point is, cunts will often chase people already in relationships. A cunt acts cuntally much as a tiger acts tigeriffically; it doesn't GUARANTEE he will one day cunt you over, but if he does, don't fucking complain—he let you know he was a cunt from the get go. So, take your cuntering like the cunt you were to let your ex be cunted by your cunt fucking cunt cunting way. *I might have lost the plot a bit here, but the point is if you know someone sometimes actively does really bad things and you choose to have them in your life then you can't complain if they continue to do bad things. PS—I am not sure if I should be editing this in a Starbucks, then again when I turned on my computer in here earlier I realized that I had several pages of pop-up porn sites to close before I could open Word. What's worse to show in public, the word cunt or pictures of them?*

By the way, I've discovered proof there is no such thing as karma; because it turns out that if you actively chase after someone else's girlfriend/wife/boyfriend/husband/etc you are NOT automatically raped in the ass by a poltergeist! *Poltergeists are always letting me down! I don't know why I keep praying to them.*

Little known fact: Some people are offended by the word 'cunt'. I know—how can that be? Yet, if you are the type of person who can be *offended* by a random assembly of letters then you automatically BECOME a cunt! Now, that's ironic. *This is where I stop being mad at something I have every right to be mad at and just start getting angry at the world, sorry!*

This isn't just my theory, by the way. That last paragraph was a word-for-word quote form a surprisingly under quoted chapter in the Koran! Why did you think those people are so pissed off all the time? They're surrounded by cunts! (Wait, the Koran is the holy text of the Ku Klux Klan isn't it? If not, I apologize greatly, plus the KKK are cunts). *I believe I was attempting humor here, not prejudice. I'd hate my misplaced hate here to take away from the impact of my well-placed hate from before.*

Also why do girls suck your balls? It's not an erogenous zone, it can't possibly be pleasurable to the girl, and it hurts if done too hard. Plus, and I know you girls want to hear this (and sorry to any guys who do like this), but when you go poo poo, sometimes it splashes up and gets the balls, and a quick wipe with toilet paper doesn't make that area anywhere near clean enough to be ready to suck. *Ahh gross imagery, my old friend.*

Oh my God, that's the end. I remembered this being way worse than it is! Yet having just done a count and I used the c-word 39 times in a few short pages. Not sure if this means I am still so upset over what happened (I am) so I don't take anything back or it's that I am so desensitized to that word (I am) that I don't even realize that this chapter is full of vile filth. Let's move on.

When I first wrote this, I guess I thought I was somehow getting them back by saying mean things. Wow, you're fucking my girlfriend and I'm anonymously calling you a cunt. I may as well challenge you to a duel and take on your machine gun with a feather—I lose and look pathetic! Wait till you fall to another trick of mine - naming rapists and murderers in my novels after people who piss me off. I'm so dastardly.

Anyway, the feeling of moving was way better than the feeling I had when writing the above piece. It's the best way to get you from where you're not meant to be to where you are meant to be, to start afresh, and to inspire new explorations and adventures.

Around two years ago I made the big decision to move to New York City to try and become a comedian. It was the best decision I ever made in my life; the first month or two there I was the happiest, most confident and full of inspiration I had ever been. Then I met this girl and we swiftly moved to LA together, had some amazing times, some awful times, and ultimately I lost track of my goals. But I can't move back to New York right now, or stay in LA. I don't have access to a visa that would let me stay for any significant period of time, so I am heading home to Australia. Even if it's not the place I'd most like to be, it is a place I truly love, it is my home and always will be, and it is full of most of my best friends, my family, and really I am looking forward to it immensely. I am not sure if I have murdered the memories from above, well, I know I haven't, but I have healed enough to be able to at least attempt to make fun of it, so that's a good thing.

So, off to Australia I go. I don't know how it will go, but I can pretty much tell you one thing for sure: if anyone hurts me along the way I'm going to totally call them a cunt!

DON'T LOOK AT ME LIKE THAT

The Los Angeles dream is officially over, and I have now been back in Sydney for forty-eight hours or so. It was Monday night last night and I felt like some action, so I headed to the local restaurant district looking for some fun.

I stopped and ate at a Thai restaurant and as I was eating my satay chicken a fat bald guy at the table next to me suddenly burst into tears. It was abrupt and seemingly unprovoked. He was apologetic, and his impossibly cute girlfriend was sweet, caring and supportive of him. I was glad; I would have hated it if she had turned out to be a bitch, then I would have had no idea how this fat loser had managed to score a girlfriend cuter than I could ever get.

I wandered around looking for a bar with some activity, and of the three local places, not one seemed to have a customer. Ahhh, Sydney, our world city, a place where if it isn't Friday night, and there are no scumbag cops and bouncers trying to antagonize people, there is no activity at all.

Note: Patriotism and optimism are my forte; hope that my abundance of these things doesn't make you feel sick.

I went to another pub which had awesome Czech beers and also often had cute bar staff due, from my understanding, to the owner's keenness for attempting to sleep with naive foreign backpackers (that bastard, I would never try to hook up with, um, I mean please bring me some new Swedish or Czech girls).

I walked in and immediately found the barman looking at me like I was a leper and telling me not to dare even think of ordering food because the kitchen was closed.

'What is going on?' I thought to myself, when I realized I was wearing a hat. A Jimi Hendrix Experience Brand funky corduroy pink old school driving type hat, thank you very much, but oh no, I had forgotten!

You see, around seven years ago I was in Austria and I found a traditional, four-hundred-year-old hat store. I bought a cool hat that looked like it had been collected after a man threw it in the air to celebrate the official end of World War One, and over the next month of travelling I got so many compliments for it I became an instant hat addict. A couple of years later and I had an awesome hat collection, one which means when I am out and about girls and boys alike frequently want to try my hat on, and often get photographed in it, and one time I even got offered a hundred dollars for a hat I'd paid twenty bucks for only hours before. I know! How cool and business savvy am I?

Another year or so on and my unique, funky and original style had been copied by so many people that I kind of lost enthusiasm for it myself. Assholes, if you *copy* style you don't *have* style, it's really kind of simple. It's like you sometimes see 'fashion experts' wearing business suits. I have known seventeen-year-old junior accountants that wear business suits. THAT IS NOT A FASHIONABLE OUTFIT, IT'S A CLICHÉD SIGN OF SHEEP-LIKE PATHETICISM! Fashion experts? Yeah right, next you'll be telling me John Bilsy from Cardiff, Wales is super fashionable because he too chooses to have a nose on his face!

Also I know! How cool must Bilsy be to get a random mention in my book? I recommend shagging him.

Also, around the time hats began to get popularized, something as scholarly as snorting urine-soaked feces happened. I started being told that hats were banned in bars and pubs in Sydney. Apparently my bright pink and green hats meant that should I choose to start a fight then it would be hard to identify me on security camera. Ahh, how intelligent - make decisions assuming people are prone to fighting rather than prone to peace, while simultaneously suggesting that wearing a hat specifically chosen to help me stand out would make it HARDER to be identified, should their undeniably stupid pre-conceived notions of me prove to be true. Yay for idiots.

AND NOW THINGS SMARTER THAN THE NO-HAT RULE By Dave

- Injecting sand into the eyes of possums in the hope that this will solve the global financial crisis
- Hosting a dinner party and using a cloud for a table
- Letting teenagers become parents
- Monitoring world terrorism movements by interrogating rocks
- Using your watch to tell the time the next meteorite will hit Jupiter
- Giving pedicures to phonebooths
- Passenger airplanes that are fueled by nightclub bouncers' intelligence

Well, you get the point—unless you're a bouncer, in which case if you're reading this (ha ha), I mean if someone is reading this to you, have them try to explain it to you, then remind them they are spending time with a bouncer, what the hell is wrong with them?

As it was, despite my forgetting the hat ban tonight, there were only two other people in this pub, so I was let in, but I was served with a rudeness which should automatically force bankruptcy. I hate to admit to something so rude, but after he took my order I thought to myself a word I would never use, 'cunt', before I chugged my beer and slunk away into the night wondering just why I had returned to Sydney.

Also, it reminded me of something—I *try* to stand out now, but ten years ago I would have spontaneously exploded a lung to avoid even a moment of standing out.

For the bulk of my life I chose clothes purely on their ability to keep me as anonymous as possible. For close to a decade I wore a navy-blue polo shirt at least four days a week. I wore plain jeans, plain shirts, plain sweaters, and plain shoes. I should have been a communist, but that would have required carrying a red flag, and red was far too fancy for the likes of me. Afterwards it was things like hats that helped me expunge myself of such a stupid lifestyle. Till the man took that away from me – 'EVERYONE MUST BE THE SAME!' Die you bastards.

When hats were banned from the nightlife, I was forced to try something else. So I bleached my hair blonde, and then began to overload it with temporary bright aqua blue, pink, purple and bright red hair dyes so I had constantly changing hair colors. Take that, normality!

Which brings me to what happened one day in Melbourne. I had my hair a lovely mostly florescent blue, with a hint of pink, color. It was winter and cold, so I was wearing multiple layers, a long white musical note ornamented scarf, and my blue and black striped fingerless gloves.

I was walking down the arty area of Brunswick Street, minding my own business, moments after a random encounter with stranger who was ecstatic that he had found his favorite brand of spray paint.

'I finally found my favorite spray paint!' he yelled at me with pure joy as he crossed the street

'Awesome,' I replied. 'Have fun doing graffiti!' I added.

Then he looked at me like I was a total weirdo, sprayed a big pile of paint into a brown paper bag, stuck his face into the bag and inhaled deep into his lungs, before returning to show me a beaming paint-covered smile.

It was after this something that *totally* unexpected happened. A guy started hitting on me!

'Do you need something to eat?' he asked.

'No, I'm cool, thanks for the offer though,' I respond.

'Do you have somewhere to sleep tonight?' he followed.

'Oh my God, this guy has jumped almost instantly from offering to buy me lunch to trying to get me to stay the night,' I thought, flattered, but heterosexual enough not to be tempted.

It was only as he kept talking that it became clear what was actually happening. He wasn't trying to pick me up, no, he was a social worker who thought I was homeless and in need of aid! It took me a good few minutes to convince him that while I was sleeping in a hostel which would turn out to be so full of bed bugs that within days I would be covered in a full galaxy of bites, and while I may look disheveled, that I was in fact financially secure.

'Does my butt look big in this?' stupid insecure girls often apparently ask.

'Do I look homeless in this?' is my now ready-to-go counter punch, should I ever find myself close to an insecure girl.

In the meantime, I was less than two days back home and getting treated poorly in an almost empty pub on a Monday night for scandalously wearing a hat. This coming home was going to take some getting used to. In the interim I was just glad I was not a fat bald guy who randomly burst into tears at random Thai restaurants. I'd hate to be comforted by a gorgeous young girl right now, or even worse, a bouncer, in which case I'd be so stupid I wouldn't be able to instantly spot the difference between a horny gay man and a benevolent social worker.

AWESOME, ANOTHER
SHITTY PROBLEM

Almost five years had passed since I lost my virginity, which made it right about time for me to finally properly have sex with a second girl and to 'make love' for the first time.

I was staying in a hostel in Nice on the French Riviera (I know, I have travelled a lot, of all the things I haven't enjoyed about my life, this is the part of my life that is the opposite of that) when my dorm room, which I had been enjoying all to myself for a few days, was suddenly filled up with an entire gaggle of Americans. I wasn't particularly happy at first; they slept all day, which at the time made them seem like pathetic wastes of tourist space to me, however my mind was quickly changed by a very special member of their group—see if you can guess? That's right, a girl!

Their group was getting dressed up for a night on the town and one of the girls, who was staying in a different room, came into our room to ask her friends if her outfit was ok. Holy christ it was! She was wearing this little red body-hugging dress, and this girl was fucking gorgeous. I couldn't take my eyes off her.

After she went back to her room to finish getting ready (and allow my erection a little break from throbbing), I got chatting with some of my new roommates and they asked me if I wanted to join them for some drinks. Even though at this stage of my life I was still a very infrequent drinker, I said yes immediately because

I wanted to be near that girl. I would have done ANYTHING to be near that girl tonight. They could have led me into a volcano and I wouldn't have seen the red lava because nothing could distract me from that red dress, plus you know, all the saliva I was drooling over the thought of what may be under it would have put out the volcano anyway.

We headed out on the town and I was walking towards the bars with the gang, a strong group of thirteen people who all turned out to be awesome, and were on a weekend break from studying in Florence. They were asking me about some of my travelling stories and I was telling a story about a strange Christian hostel where I stayed in Norway, when another girl from the group, Janey, inspired by my story, made a bee-line to talk to me.

From the moment we first start chatting we did not stop. For hours we talked. It was one of those rare moments where we just clicked. She was really beautiful but, more than that, our conversation was so sweet and captivating that I somehow forgot all about the red dress girl.

Janey and I ended up leaving the group to go for a walk, before we sat down by the water on the rocky Nice beach, and after I told her some bizarre theory about how I think African Americans should be proud of their slave names because these are the names their ancestors carried as they fought for freedom and equality, she decided she wanted to kiss me under the moonlight.

This wasn't just a random hook up. This was love.

I woke her up (in her bed in a separate room from where I slept) the next morning with chocolate croissants and orange juice, and from then on we barely spent two seconds not kissing, cuddling, holding hands or just having great conversation, as we spent a wonderful yet brief and oh-so-romantic time together enjoying the French Riviera. A couple of weeks later we would re-unite in Florence, and fall completely in love with each other over pasta, art, and Tuscany. After less than seven days of actually being in the same country as each other, she took me to the opera, we cuddled all night, and after I kissed her on her doorstep we said 'I love you' to each other. It was the first time I had ever exchanged those words with another human being, and this was without the slightest exaggeration or doubt the happiest time of my entire life.

I was on a whirlwind backpacking tour, with lots of plans already made, so I invited her to come with me north to Switzerland and come see the Alps with me and she agreed. We were now saying 'I love you' a hundred times a day. We were mentally projecting into a future together. And as we made plans for Switzerland we decided to book our first night together in a private room. We'd been living separately in hostels and group homes up till now, so a private room would bring us something important, *privacy*, and with us both agreeing out loud that we should get a private room, we both knew what was inevitable—it was sex! Although, even now looking back on it, even in my mid freaking twenties, I still didn't really believe it was going to happen.

We checked in after a long train ride, and went for a bite to eat and a beer at the bar. We got chatting with a stranger, but while holding hands under the table and looking into each others' eyes, we both knew this was not a time we wanted to make new friends, and we made an excuse and headed for the bedroom.

We began making out, saying how much we loved each other with both words and touch, and here, in this beautiful moment, with snow-capped mountains out of the window like a story from a 1940s movie, I was about to discover something new about myself.

Even with a girl I am in love with, when romance and good feelings are way more at play than raw horniness, I am quite capable of cumming on the very first stroke, during the actual penetration while making love. Holy shit.

I was mortified with embarrassment. All the splendor I had been feeling for days drained out of my body, and all I could think was, 'I'm being judged', 'she is going to change her mind about me' and 'she'll never have sex with me again, and if SHE won't, then no one ever, ever will.'

I couldn't possibly bring myself to confess what I had just done. So instead I once again did something monumentally stupid, and continued to make love to her while wearing a full condom. I pumped away, hoping she somehow didn't notice, only now with a new plan, I needed to cum again pretty quickly, so I could apologize for still being fast without confessing just how fast I was, but get out of there so we didn't end up with a burst condom on our hands. It would be kind of hard to explain that the condom broke, and was full of semen, even though I hadn't let her know I had climaxed.

Now I had two new problems:

1. While still raging hard, I was nowhere near another orgasm. A pattern has immerged in even my briefest of sex lives, wanting not to orgasm makes me blow instantly, needing to cum makes it harder to cum than to fit a watermelon in my penis hole.
2. She has now also had an orgasm, and is making it clear that she is no longer enjoying this and is ready for me to finish.

I consider faking an orgasm, which I figure will be easy to get away with seeing as I do have a condom full of semen to show as evidence. But I didn't know how to fake an orgasm, and I was way too scared of being caught, this was the love of my life, I needed to be convincing in a way that I would then be able to repeat in future love making. So I came (ha ha—pun) up with a new plan, a change of position, then while we moved awkwardly around I pretended the condom had slid off so I better put a new one on. Brilliant! A little bit of sleight of hand, so she didn't see a condom full in only the way a man in his mid-twenties having sex for only the fifth time, and who has spent the past four months living in hostel dorms where finding the privacy to 'clean the pipes' is extremely hard to do. As I rolled over and out of her, I got a look at the condom; this thing looked like an over filled water balloon.

But she didn't notice (read—almost certainly did and was so monumentally weirded out by me at this stage that she was just going to go with it and try and make some goddamn sense of it some other time) and I whipped on another condom with lightning speed and got right back inside her.

We now had about ten minutes of horrible sex, with me apologizing constantly, and completely unable to cum and her having about as much fun as a caged hen. I eventually realized that I could simply not continue with this, and so I stopped and made some other excuse and escaped to the bathroom, where I tried to finish myself off on my own, and still failed.

I have never felt more shame, and less self-confidence, in my life.

If this had been a one-night stand I probably would have given up on sex for life. I mean, I hated it, and more than that, I literally took my penis out of a vagina only to switch to using my hand alone in the bathroom. Clearly this sex thing just was not something for me. But this wasn't a one-night stand. This was my first love. We spent the night cuddling, her sleeping, me lying awake wondering if she would say in the morning, 'I'm sorry, but I forgot about this thing in Florence so I have to go, but I'll email you sometime, you know, when I have some free time, like when I get back to America, for example, or after I graduate college. Then again, I am doing a seven-year degree, and the job market after that is going to be hard and time consuming, and oh shit that's my train, got to ru.....'. Instead, the next morning we went for breakfast, and she still kept telling me she loved me and holding me close, and then we headed to a tiny village halfway up a mountain together, where the lady who ran the bed and breakfast we stayed at was convinced we'd been together for years and would be together forever.

In the course of my relationship with Janey, some discoveries were to be made. I liked this love dealy, and I did not want it to end, although I could never stop doubting every single little tiny freaking thing about it. We had one little fight and I was sure it was the end. We had a slight difference of opinion over something and I beat myself up over it obsessively. Also, I was a chronic premature ejaculator, yet this left me far from satisfied and I never wanted sex to be even close to over once this happened. She, on the other hand, always came after about thirty seconds and all sexual contact after that was horrible for her. She hated foreplay, while I had barely even heard of it, and wanted to explore as much as possible. Basically, I was mental, we lived in different countries and we were about as sexually compatible as a chair and a rotary telephone.

After Switzerland, we separated again for a couple of weeks then met back up in Munich for another brief time together, and as I said goodbye to her as we climbed on different trains heading in different directions, I cried the hardest I ever cried in my life. With nothing but a cap she had bought me as a present to shield my face and my shame from my fellow passengers.

We stayed in touch for the next year, never really discussing our plans, even though while in Europe I had told her I would try to move to America to be with her. I mentioned it occasionally but she never really seemed too enthusiastic about the prospect. But then her mum offered to buy her plane tickets to Australia. She came to visit and it was like Switzerland again, for about eight seconds. I wanted to show her the best time possible so I took time off work and took her on an immensely expensive holiday to an all five-star island resort with both plane and helicopter flights over the Great Barrier Reef, she wanted to let me know we were just friends.

With a couple of days left on her visit, she suddenly went totally cold on me, wouldn't let me touch her or barely look at her, and then made it clear, with no reason given, that this was the end for us, and while my heart lay on the floor with her every footstep crushing it one more step closer to death, she took pity on me, looked up at me and asked if I could take her shopping so I could follow through on my promise to buy souvenirs for all her friends and family.

Fuck me, why didn't I just hit on the hot girl in the gorgeous red dress?

LIKE THAT'S THE END
OF THAT STORY

Three years crawled by after Janey left. From recollection I didn't touch a girl the entire time. I definitely didn't have sex. I found myself twenty-seven years old, I had only had sex about twelve times in my life, I was lonely as all hell, my period of backpacking and exploring the world was over, and I was now ensconced in a career I had known since birth I would now be in until death, and hating every single micro-second of it, and my depression became so severe that I hit a point where I had absolutely nothing left in my soul.

Two options ran around in my head. I could finally kill myself or I could go to the doctor and ask to be medicated with antidepressants, something I promised myself I never, ever would do. Killing myself seemed like the logical, easiest, least depressing, least scary, and least humiliating option. It was time. I had nothing left to live for.

Surprisingly, I don't know how or why, and thank God, thank Buddha, thank Allah, thank the little chirpy bird in the tree, thank Mother Nature, or whoever the fuck, or whatever the fuck the higher power is for influencing me, I somehow talked myself into choosing the pills. And honestly, fuck you Xenu, Tom Cruise and the rest of you evil imbecilic Scientologist whack jobs that go around denouncing psychology and anti-depression medication. Seriously - Fuck you. If not for that shit, I would be DEAD! I have zero doubt about it. Instead, I have learned to LOVE to be alive. I have learned to LOVE life. I have been on countless amazing adventures, met amazing people, and I have used my new-found happiness and energy for life to enrich other people's lives. I know this because I get hundreds (exaggeration) of emails from strangers telling me how much I have inspired them. All you cunts do is ruin art, make people doubt that humans are the most intelligent life form on earth, and if anyone who was like me has listened to you, then you have quite literally killed people! Fuck YOU!

Having said that, there is one particular side effect from these little pills that has had none but a small negative influence on my life since I began taking them.

Let's first look at the good. With the chemical balance in my brain being artificially boosted, I began to feel immediately happier and more confident. This had a wonderful run-on effect. I had already begun to write, but now I began to have faith in my writing, and felt that it was a genuine career possibility. This made me feel good. Suddenly nothing was pre-ordained for me anymore; the possibilities were endless. My first novel started to pour out of me, and I was proud of it, so much so that when I would meet people, especially girls, I wanted to tell them about it.

It was in this period of my life I discovered the magical three ingredients to hooking up with girls:

1. Be making craploads of money, and making this clear with expensive suits and generous spending habits
2. When asked about how you made this money, spend almost no time going over the boring details of working in a corporate job, and instead tell them about your actual passion—being an artist
3. Have these girls for the most part be backpackers, so they are loose and have a traveler's spirit of adventure, and allowing you not to give the slightest shit where it is going other than an attempt to get their panties off and if they say no then moving onto their friend

In all truthfulness, I began to get laid occasionally, and as I have pointed out before, getting laid gives you the confidence to try and get laid more, and girls are most attracted to confidence, which means they'll have sex with you, which in no time at all leads you to becoming an absolute asshole.

I have often referred to this period in my life as my 'purple patch'. For about nine months I had a couple of back to back fuck buddies (not literally), or 'Benches' as I'd call them, because I would try to meet other chicks and if I failed I'd pull a girl off the reserves bench. And I got so confident and cocky about hitting on girls I would do it anywhere, from bars, to clubs, on trains, at shops and just on the street.

Now, don't get me wrong, I got turned down a LOT. But the hits came just often enough that I could be turned down three hundred times and still have hope for lucky lady 301.

Before you get to ahead of yourself, I want you to know two things.

1. I treated girls like shit in this brief period, and I hated doing that, so much so that well before a year had passed I couldn't do it anymore and as soon as I started treating girls sweetly and cared about their feelings again, the sex disappeared and has never come back
2. There is another horrible side effect to anti-depressants — they make it almost impossible to orgasm

At first this was brilliant. One of my biggest fears when meeting a girl was that if I ever did get to have sex with her, my brutal premature ejaculation would come out to play and I would be immediately dumped, humiliated and crushed. It was worth being celibate to avoid that. Now I could last, and last, and last, and last, and sometimes have sex for hours without a single orgasm, and the girls never seemed to give the slightest shit I had made them cum seventy-four times but missed out myself, and this helped me not feel bad for using them for sex.

It was way better to have sex six times in just one month and get to orgasm one of those times than go multiple years without having sex at all. But this didn't last. Now that I actually got to have sex, the thrill of actually getting to have sex went away and I wanted to now try actually *enjoying* sex. Thus, the problems again arise, good sir. As we have established, trying to cum makes it harder to cum, and girls DO notice when you start getting frustrated and angry with yourself for this inability. I began making excuses like I'd had too much to drink, or my favorite: 'I had a bunch of small ones that happen without ejaculate'—which even I don't know the real meaning of.

A couple of months into this embarrassing memory murdering, I knew there were some big things about myself I wanted to repair. I am heading into my mid thirties now, and my pathetic sex life has the added bonus of the reality that even the sex I've had for the most part has been awful and orgasm free, and if I ever wanted to enjoy this apparently wonderful aspect of life, I needed to take a big risk and go off antidepressants.

I had actually tried going off once before—the wrong way, cold turkey—and within days it had rendered me a bitter, miserable mess. This time I needed to do it smart and wean myself off slowly for a long time. As of the time of writing, it has been four months since I started this process. My original habit was two to three pills a day, and I worked down to two a day, then three every two days, then one a day, until now where it's one a week or so. And to put it bluntly, my penis has burst back to life like a coked-up zombie. It literally shakes with delight at even the thought of a fully dressed girl. I am not exaggerating here. This thing spends its days throbbing, leaking, and acting like an ADD kid on seven liters of red creaming soda. At its absolute calmest it's like an idling truck. If this thing gets even close to a vagina anytime soon, I am worried he will explode like a suicide bomber, and I don't mean as in he'll explode with an orgasm, but literally explode as in be torn head to shaft to base in a million bloody pieces splashed across the wall, leaving me with a bloody stump. I don't think there is another thing on earth as hyperactive as my penis is right now.

Suffice to say, if I actually do get laid anytime soon, I will definitely have an orgasm. But it won't be when we have sex, it will from her brushing her hand over my back, or smiling at me, and the orgasm will take place entirely in snug underpants. And frankly, if she still wants to sleep with me after that, she may well be a keeper.

I think I'm safe, though. I am still unable to treat girls like an asshole, so they'd still rather fuck scumbags like Tom Cruise—fuck you, Xenu.

Update:

1. Holy shit, I seriously can't believe that I managed to miss that I was also extremely negative, angry, bitter, and self-hating during this period. I don't know what the solution is for me, but going off anti-depressants on my own, with no professional help, or even a loving friend or girlfriend watching over me and boosting my mood is not it.
2. Man I really, truly was obsessed with sex this year, wow, I'm surprised I didn't end up associating awfully non-sexual things like terrorism and suicide to sex, oh wait, I did.
3. I blame Tom Cruise.

CRACK!

I don't really remember my voice breaking. I didn't do the squeaky thing, it just kind of got lower over a period of time, a nice slow burn, which for most puberty-riddled boys would be a cool relief, but in my case as you may be able to guess, my voice didn't even START breaking until I was well into university, so I was well past being thankful for any luck in that department.

Yes, college isn't *necessarily* a place of sexual exploration for all of us.

Other things I didn't like about my university days were my classmates, my subjects, my torturous shyness, my nick name 'Doogie Howser'. My classmates actually thought I was a 12-year-old genius who had come to university really young, so it really baffled them when my grades were all awful, but what else could they think? Actually, in hindsight, they could have thought I had some sort of rare anti-aging disease, which I guess is kind of true. How dare you tease someone for that! I of course also hated my exams, my workload, my inability to concentrate while studying, meaning I had to do way more of that than I should have had to, my commute to and from school (which on many occasions I did while crying in the car), the thoughts going through my brain all day, and every other little thing.

Oh wait, no, over the course of a couple of weeks in class I taught myself how to do that Star Trek finger split salute, that's kind of cool!

On the other hand, I did once get caught masturbating my still completely underdeveloped penis in the front seat of my car by a school security guard. I have since learned it's advised NOT to masturbate directly below a security camera. I am convinced the footage will be on the Internet one day, although in my defense, see the rest of this book. By the way, I am not sure when I would consider my penis to have finally reached full maturity. But on one joyful day approaching the very end of my teens, I suddenly realized I could now masturbate with more than two fingers! Yay.

On orientation day for university I suddenly encountered a group of people handing out free condoms to new students. They were handing them out indiscriminately, and just the thought that my new classmates were already possibly sexually active was painful enough for me for this experience to be horrible, that is until a man looked up ready to hand me a package, before a pause, then a massive public display of awkward humiliation as this man clearly had an internal debate as to which of the following were true:

1. I was a new student
2. I was someone's kid brother
3. I was an eighteen-year-old with a weird non-aging genetic disorder
4. I was a 12-year-old kid genius

Then, while pondering those four possibilities, he also had to decide whether it was weirder and more embarrassing to:

1. Hand me condoms in front of fifty (thousand) people all thinking the same thing: 'No god damn way that kid needs condoms' (I wasn't just young, but fat and ugly too)
2. Say to me out loud, 'You clearly have no use for these products, so piss off.'
3. Drop his products on the floor and run away.
4. Say, 'Sorry, man, If I give out condoms to a 12-year-old I might get arrested.

It was, perhaps surprisingly, quite excruciating.

I guess he chose snake eyes, 1 and 1, and so he handed them to me, as the crowd looked on in disbelief and with an air of disgust at the obvious rainforest-bulldozing-like waste of giving them to someone such as I.

It was orientation day - I had yet to have even my first ever day at what would be my home for the next three and a half years - and I was already convinced that every time I spoke to any of my peers for my entire time at the school, as soon as I left they would turn to each other, burst into laughter and say, 'Ha HA! Like that dude will ever need a condom!'

Well, joke's on them, because what these bastards didn't know of course is that within two years I was to roll one of these very condoms onto my penis, and when it stayed put and was subsequently filled with my masturbation-induced jizz, I finally, FINALLY, received what to me was the confidence-boosting proof that if by some fluke I ever got close enough to a girl that she may accidently brush my crotch region where she was sure to find my pretty much permanent erection, that she'd find a man-sized penis, and I wouldn't have to quickly make up some weird disease! Yes, that actual free condom became one of the greatest gifts ever given to me! So, hell yeah, joke's on you, you doubting wankers.

Oh, I also once used the lube he gave me in that package to curiously stick a hairbrush handle up my ass, and finally learn the lesson I don't like having sex with hair care paraphernalia. 'This kid doesn't need a free condom and lube package, my ass!' (damn you, pun.) Later on, just to confess it all for some reason, my self-exploration and curiosity would find me masturbating one day with my legs above my head so I could cum in my own face.

Also for the record the answer is I only WISH I were gay! Seriously! Oh my God, all those years of wondering, 'What the hell is so wrong and different about me?' could be washed away with a simple, 'Oh, I like cock, that explains it,' followed by a life where it's a million times easier to get laid, garnished with no fear of unwanted pregnancy (yet another thought that won't leave my plague-riddled brain during coitus). How could you not desire that? Well, actually, being bi would be gold. You're out with a male and female friend. 'You guys see anyone of the opposite sex that's hot? Because you can both let me know, I'll gladly fuck either. Oh yeah, bisexual in the house, motherfuckers!'

Cut to many years later and after returning to Australia for a brief time renewing my US visa, I decided to hit one of my favorite nights out in Sydney. My favorite music venue, Spectrum, on Thursday nights throws open the fire escapes to link up with four other adjacent nightclubs and fill it to the rafters full of young hipsters, emos, metal heads, and all around alternative people for their awesome 'Hot Damn' night.

I had only been back in the country for a couple of days and I had completely forgotten that the beer is way stronger in Australia than in America, plus partying on my own always makes me drink faster because it both keeps my hands and mind busy and helps build up the extra confidence it takes to talk to random girls wingman-less.

A few hours later I was ridiculously drunk, and wisely decided for my own safety that I should head home. I got to the train station and the big board told me I had 25 minutes to wait for the next train.

Next thing I noticed was a train is pulling up to the platform. 'Thank God, home in twenty minutes then bedtime,' I thought before looking up and seeing the doors open and scores of people dressed in business suits and work attire pour out of the train. 'Holy shit, it isn't twenty minutes later, it's the next morning! What the fuck have I done?'

I looked at my watch, it was worse than I thought.

The hour hand was pointing between the eight and the nine, and the minute hand was right on the seven. It was over eight hours after I had arrived on the train platform! Three hours after the trains had begun running. Literally hundreds of people, if not thousands, had seen my pathetic drunk ass sleeping on the platform. This was Town Hall Station, right smack bang in the very heart of the Sydney Central Business District. I could easily have stumbled onto the tracks. I should absolutely have been arrested and thrown in the drunk tank at the local police station, or at the very least been ejected and forced to get a cab home, and it would have been all my own idiotic fault, clearly.

Yet, keep in mind for a moment that this is a train station with no garbage bins for 'security' reasons (apparently if terrorists come to the station with a bomb and don't find a trash can to put it in, they go home, decide to quit Al Qaeda and take up childcare for a living).

Three things to point out right now:

1. I am an enormous fool
2. The garbage bins are NOT the problem with the security at Town Hall train station in Sydney
3. Having now once again returned to Australia, I was ready to jump headfirst back into strong-ass Aussie beer, and fun nights out.

Lo and behold, good sir, for my first proper party night out upon my return to Sydney, I grabbed some friends (safety in numbers) and headed back to Hot Damn, and hot damn it if on the way in there are not strange people handing out little packs of condoms and lube, and as I am about to enter, the girl looks up at me and says, 'Do you need two packs?' (Safety in numbers!)

No, she didn't really say that, but there was not even a hint of 'oh my God what do I do, what do I do?' on her face, instead she looked at me and thought 'there is nothing about him that would make handing him condoms humiliating for me or him.' Hell yeah there isn't, now where do I get a hairbrush?

VANDALAY INDUSTRIES

Ah condoms, protector of lack of parenthood, numbing instrument of sexual pleasure, defender of STDs, and if you're like me, provider of some of the least fun moments of your life, i.e. going through your toiletry bag and realizing that the twenty-four pack of condoms you bought a few years ago have now passed their expiration date and there are still twenty-four in the pack.

I have had to throw out expired condoms way too many times in my life. I like to be prepared but sometimes preparation comes back to bite you on your 'oh my God, it's once again been *years* since I have been laid' ass. It happened again to me recently. The condoms I bought when I was dating my ex expired, and my all-too-brief entries back into the game have barely made a dent in the box.

This is a shit feeling.

Truth is, I am feeling awful at the moment. I am missing friends, the art scene and the nightlife of LA. I am missing the antidepressants in my blood stream. My home is not feeling as homely as it used to, and I am remembering that I have not stuck onto my new 'celebrate EVERYTHING' mantra from earlier in the year. That was supposed to be a new way of life, why did I drop this?

I had just thrown a big pack of condoms in the trash (some of my really old expired ones are kept in a place specifically to test whether people will steal someone else's condoms, because if they do, then I say they deserve faulty ones. Is that wrong of me?) Well, screw that, I only looked at the old box because I was adding brand new ones to the stack, free ones I was given last week, and this meant I knew where I could get more free replacements, and remember that most people don't have the inclination, the good fortune or the balls to live how I do, 'So shut your mouth you whiney loser Dave and celebrate it all.'

It was time for another night where I go out and simply remember to celebrate absolutely everything, big or small. Yay! Here goes:

I left the house just in time to see a super cute neighbor come into the building wearing a beautiful blue summer dress and instead of being annoyed that she already has one of those kid things and probably a husband dealy, I celebrated that those kid things keep boring married folk at home and leave the bars full of horny young singles.

With a celebratory skip in my step, I walked right onto a train I would have missed with a somber stroll, and as I arrived in the city I saw a girl fall over due to her silly high-heeled shoes and I got to celebrate being way smarter than anyone who would wear such stupid footwear.

As I walked towards the club, I saw scores of hipster-type boys heading in the same direction and got to celebrate my free natural stride as they walked uncomfortably in ball-crushing skinny jeans.

By the way, playing this game can make you sometimes come across as perhaps a tiny bit cynical or mean, but it's not. It's merely enjoying finding the good in any situation for you personally rather than finding negativity in other people's idiosyncrasies. It's a fine line but an utterly enjoyable one. Speaking of lines, this positive attitude allowed me to see the line of the club full of hot girls and not get all negative about the wait but rather actually celebrate that there were hot girls!

Free condoms pocketed on the way in, I hopped up the stairs to the club, and basked with the joy of a man returning to a familiar and well-loved place knowing a fun night was ahead.

First band that played was such a load of clichéd screamo death metal bollocks that I was able to celebrate knowing if and when I started my next band, our worst ever gig will be way better than their best ever.

And now to celebrate things that are more unique and therefore better than screamo metal:

- Ducks that shoot razor blades from their beaks
- Purple pool cues at $1709 a dozen
- B.O. (smells better, too)

I celebrated my way through a beer, then another, then a couple more, plus a Jager-bomb, and celebrated how none of the girls I was trying to smile at would even look at me, leaving me free to celebrate knowing I still had the option of meeting way nicer girls later, before celebrating writing down the famous last words of a celebrator:

'There are so many hot girls here tonight I'd be happy to hook up with *ANYONE*!'

I celebrated a self-reminder that I desire to be a fearless performer and for some reason this made me celebrate a weird note I wrote down 'celebrate being a fearless casual observer'.

Having confused myself with that thought, I reminded myself that coming to places like this alone was way more gutsy than pathetic, and that was totally worth celebrating.

So I jumped up on the stage, which had now been converted into a dance floor, allowing me the rare thought 'I am celebrating that the bands are *finished*?' and as I looked out over the crowd dancing below I was reminded just how 'right' and 'at home' I feel when I am on stage with an audience before me, as is always the case when I am in front of a crowd. So I celebrated spending a couple of hours of massaging my own ego in my head, trying to remind myself that I am good and talented and to go for it more often, while I celebrated dancing in a crazy, half serious, half humorous, half mental way, as I like to do, more to attract attention than anything else.

With my adrenalin pumping, and a small box of brand new condoms filling up my pocket, I celebrated the start of the-hitting-on-some-girls phase of the evening and kept reminding myself I was supposed to be celebrating as one by one they rejected me.

One girl who was wearing a funky hat came over and switched hats with my funky hat, and then another dude came over and returned my hat to my head then whispered in my ear 'only if you want STDs dude' and I'm not sure if I celebrated that.

With options already starting to fade, I walked towards the bar for another drink and an investigation mission, and coming my way I saw a drunk-as-fuck girl who shopped at 'This Is Even Too Slutty For Hookers Secret'. I made an effort to give her a wide berth but she stumbled and fell into me anyway, and even though I tried to get out of the way, and then saved her from her drunk ass falling all the way to the ground, she repaid me by *shoving me* and mumbling, 'Get your hands off me' and I fought really, really hard to figure out what to celebrate and decided upon the thought that some guy would almost certainly have sex with her tonight, and celebrating that it wouldn't be *me* cleaning her vomit out of my sheets half way through the night.

I continued to be rejected by more girls and now getting too drunk myself to really maintain my joyful outlook on life, I celebrated wisely going home.

The next day I woke up at the crack of 1pm and celebrated realizing that had one of the many girls who rejected me last night said yes instead, right now I'd be trying to get a 'regret' to go home and/or figuring out which pawn shop my laptop was currently for sale at.

So I celebrated the silliness of the male outlook on sex, and then celebrated the joy of knowing I have a four pack of fresh new condoms with three years to go before getting sad at throwing them out unused.

This celebration dealy really is awesome; I recommend it to all! Then again, if you instead just have a significant other, a wife or husband, boyfriend or girlfriend who you love, I won't mind if you go ahead and just celebrate that instead, and if you need a condom I have a 'special' batch hidden away just for people like you, you healthy sex-enjoying bastards!

THE BEAR AND THE
LEAD PAINT

Speaking of celebrating and not giving a shit about what people think of me, I should point out that this new fancy don't-give-a-shit attitude lasted about three hours, then I was back to being a self-doubting neurotic twat. Maybe it doesn't matter how much you try and change yourself, maybe who you are is down to your core, and so instead why not just try and change everyone else?

Now, let me say off the bat here, that I have no recollection of any of my boy-scout masters treating me with even the slightest hint of inappropriateness. I don't have even a tiny fluff of bad memories from that place. I joined because the scout hall had awesome floors to skateboard on and stayed because the games were fun, earning badges was rewarding and the uniforms were as sexy as all hell.

The problem is that I was in that organization for a *long time* and I basically don't have ANY memories or recollections of being there. Isn't that one of the signs? That blocking out memories of a significant part of my childhood perhaps suggests that my underdeveloped youthful mind faced something so traumatic and hard to understand that my brain, rather than trying to decipher what this means, instead said, 'just chuck this one in that dark place up the back of the head near the neck, can't be assed to figure this out!' Perhaps including experiences that may explain why now at my more advanced stage of existence, 90% of my lifetime orgasms have taken place alone while watching weird types of porn?

I hope not. Every now and again I have the need to tie a knot, and I KNOW I learned how and don't remember! I'd hate to think that I lost this valuable skill because of some pesky pedophiliac scout master bastard!

Ha ha, see what I did there? I suggested that the *worst* thing about being sexually abused might be forgetting how to tie knots! Of course, the best thing is that in the future you can get away with anything.

News: Jeffery Ebens was convicted today of murdering three high school cheerleaders.

People: That's outrageous; sentence the scumbag to death!

News continued: Jeffery Ebens has been in and out of the court system since he was fifteen, after a series petty crimes that began when he ran away from home to escape years of sexual abuse.

People continued: Wait, what? Oh my God, it's not his fault, let him go, he's suffered enough (now sobbing), *he's suffered enough*!

Ha ha, see what I did there, I suggested I may one day need to be forgiven for murdering cheerleaders, ha ha! Oh my God, Dave, switch topics immediately, please!

For a long, long time, I was too nice. I was completely selfless, severely surrenderingly over-the-top nice. So nice that it made people not like me, because I never had an opinion, I never made a decision, and I was always so worried about pleasing everyone around me that I never got anything I wanted and also annoyed everyone around me, who always had to make all the decisions.

I recall one minor example out of millions of similar situations when I was on a long multi-hour train ride with a few friends and the train was so packed that we didn't all get a seat. So I volunteered to sit on the extremely uncomfortable armrest. Time and time again on this ride one of my three friends volunteered to switch places for stints and I utterly refused. It was niceness to the point of selfishly protecting my niceness no matter how stupid. This is how I *always* lived. I'm nice until it pisses people off or until I get taken advantage of.

The truth, of course, is that my selflessness was pure selfishness. I was controlling my outcomes by denying myself the options and I was denying people around me the option of being the nice one. I have since learned how irritating it is to be around people like this, and I am still like this too often. In the right balance, having someone be nice to you is amazingly nice, and doing something nice for others can make you feel like you've just eaten a nice sundae with warm butterscotch syrup sprinkled with nice. There is a pure pleasure to be found in niceness, and all it takes is for someone to offer it and another person to be grateful for it.

One of the few things I *do* remember from my time in the scouts is that I rocketed up the leadership positions within our area at speeds that I recall being considered unheard of. I choose to believe that this was not due to some sort of blocked out 'casting couch' type dealy, and rather a symptom of my God-given, undeniable natural leadership skills.

This instinct was present in me from a young age. At school sports I was always promoted to captain of my teams, and I recall often being seen as a go-to guy for wisdom in schoolyard-type disputes, or to make up stories of my grandfather's pet miniature tornado. It wasn't a choice; it was a natural inclination.

Over the years this quality was driven away, spat on and nipple twisted out of me through years of self-loathing and bullying, but it has never died. In high school even though I was too scared to talk to even my oldest friends, I took on coaching a junior basketball team, and I even played for them because I looked younger than most of the four year younger kids I coached and for some reason I didn't have a problem with being a horrible cheat back then. I continued to play sport throughout my 20s and again gravitated to captaincy and leadership, and would often give passionate half-time speeches only to be too shy to go for a beer with the boys after the game. Regardless of my flaws, my deep desire to lead has been one consistent theme in my life.

So, I sit here in Sydney, Australia, being a frustrating, whiny and unpatriotic bitch. I can complain or I can lead, and I want to lead, for god's sake. Do it or else the probably non-existent pedophiles in my scout troupe win! I *won't* let something *non-existent* beat ME! Maybe it's time for me to murder a memory in a way that helps not just me, but lots of people.

I have long been upset with all the negativity in the world. As humans in the Western world, we are overwhelmed with daily negative information. Everything from the news, to the general selfish nature of how many if not most people go about their days, to the simple fact that everywhere you look there are signs telling us what we're not allowed to do. It frustrates me and weighs on me. And before you say 'having a negative thought *about* that just adds to the problem', you should know I have actually done something about it.

I once conceived a street art project where I would go around sticking up positive street signs adjacent to all the negative ones. Next to 'No Parking Here Anytime' I could put up 'Thinking of kittens allowed here at all times' and to counter 'no shirt, no shoes, no service' I could put up 'it's hot and sunny, hell yeah!' I would have gone through with this project too, if only it was easy to make signs the same as the local traffic authority, and I could figure out how not to get arrested for it, and if it didn't make me look like a hippy twat.

I did, on the other hand, start the blog I called 'The Perfectly Positive Bear', where I tried to find the positive sides of even hugely negative news stories, things like (as suggested above): 'Experts say sexual abuse is on the rise, which is good news for future criminals, as you may have a really forgivable excuse!' And 'There is still no peace on earth, which is good news for gun owners; you may still get to shoot someone legally. I even posted TWO whole entries of The Bear.

Well, I decided I was ready for a new project in positivity. Wading through my embarrassing past is reminding me just how often people have failed to be nice to me, so why not try and encourage niceness? I needed to pull out my leadership skills and rectify this.

I came up with a genius plan. There is a website and book series out there dedicated to secrets. The idea is people send in postcards and emails anonymously revealing a secret. It is fascinating and often heartbreaking. Stories of infidelity are frequent, so are thoughts of suicide, and things like 'my husband doesn't know he isn't our son's biological father, it is really his best friend' are riveting in all their horror. It is a fun site to gaze over for a few minutes here and there, and it often leaves you moved or left deep in often depressing thought. It is amazing how affecting small bites of truth can be.

Well what if there was a place like this, where you could go, especially anytime you are feeling down, or having negative thoughts about the world, and you could get a simple short, real-life reminder that there are awesome people and situations out there? I thought it would be wonderful. So I started a facebook page dedicated to acts of niceness. The idea was that anyone could post, and should post anything nice they could say about anyone or anything. Over time, as more and more people joined, there would be an ongoing and continuously updating list of pure niceness in a way that could combat any bombardment of negativity in the world. It'd be the perfect place for a quick glance after three hours of war coverage on CNN, or after struggling in to work on a Monday morning.

I created it, went live, advertised it all over social media, encouraged people to spread the word, and began to add a bunch of my own tales of niceness to get the ball rolling. A world of niceness had begun.

As a few people added themselves to the site I began to swell with pride. This was going to be huge. I titled the page 'if I get a million fans on this page it'd be kinda nice' (this was during the phase where things like toilet brushes were getting a million fans to prove some tool could get a toilet brush a million fans) and I soon became convinced a million would be super underestimating it, and that in the way smiling at someone can spread a smile, this may actually cause people to do random acts of niceness, maybe even in the hope they'd see it come up on the page. As I said, being nice makes you feel good, having someone be nice to you makes you feel good, how could this fail?

This failed like an attempt to nap while someone chainsaws your face off. I got how many followers? Sixty-nine. Of all numbers, I hit that and stuck there, not going up or down for months, it just stuck there, like some cruel cosmic dirty joke. And after dozens of posts by me, some that were very nicely received, how many people did I find willing to say something nice about anything at all? Zero. Big fat donut! Yep, this scout leadership-climbing, pedophile-joking, overly nice author here is not enough to combat all the negativity in the world, or even some of it. I was a failure, but then again I was nice enough to try.

I'm still nice. I hold doors open; I let people off the train before I try to get on. I let people in front of me in traffic and say thank you when others do similar things for me. How am I the exception rather than the rule? Still, I can't always blame people. For some reason, some people take niceness the wrong way. Personally, I blame the people who are only *pretending* to be nice when in reality they want to do something evil. They suck, those guys.

Actually, true story: A couple of years ago I was sitting in a park near my place when a little lost boy was crying near a road and I didn't go and help him because I was worried that long-haired bearded scruffy me would be frowned upon going up to a strange boy. I kept a close eye on him so he wouldn't get into any danger, while keeping an eye out for his parents and/or someone else helping him, in frankly a park adjacent to a busy café, full of selfish and/or unobservant and/or worried about being labeled pedophiles people. It was so sad. When the dad finally showed up he seemed unconcerned his two year old had been lost next to a busy road for ten minutes and I was concerned that he was allowed to be a parent and also concerned that I was the only one that was concerned.

Three concerns don't make a right.

The Perfectly Positive Bear: Single men going anywhere near stranger children cause you to risk being called a pedophile, which is good news for men who enjoy watching small kids being hit by cars—you're now *required* to simply watch!

On the other hand, the other day I saw a heavily pregnant woman helping up an old lady who had fallen down. There is still hope.

Speaking of hope:

- If you even just work for a company that deals in computer spam, I hope you're killed by a public, spontaneous and extremely vicious pigeon attack.
- Don't take this the wrong way, but if you believe every hair has a soul, I really hope you're not also my teenage daughter because it'd be a nasty surprise to discover I had a teenage daughter, and based on my sexual history, would require the invention of time machines.
- Did you just go aawwwww? In which case I hope you just saw something cute, or gross! Or both, like a kitten pooping on a puppy.
- And if you see something nice I hope you tell someone about it, it might just catch on!

•

WHY DO YOU KEEP HITTING YOURSELF?

As may be clear by now, the worst enemy I have ever had is myself. I have deeply instilled passion for ruining things for myself. I have never been someone who fears the worst. On the contrary, for the most part I have always *prayed* for the worst. I fantasize about the people I care about dying, I daydream about everything I own catching on fire, and I romanticize over everything I have worked for collapsing around me. It's not that I enjoy pain, it's that I have so often felt it for no good reason that being given a reason is like a gift. Truth is, throughout my long battle with depression, being given a valid excuse for misery was something I craved relentlessly. Happiness was far too implausible, but warranted misery was something even I could work towards.

That's not moxy either; I literally worked towards it. Without death or disease to hang my hat on, I would instead write myself essays detailing every reason I felt I warranted misery. I was proud of this ability. I kept these essays for years like trophies. I know I still have them somewhere, I can't find them to quote from, but I was a genius at never missing a single moment that I could detest myself over. There was never the slightest intent to heal; it was unadulterated need to fuel my pain fire.

For many years the one thing I did allow to externally poke and pull at my emotions was my deep unrequited love for the North

Sydney Bears Rugby League team, a team most famous for their own seven-decade passion for failure. While most hardcore sports fans allowed the ups and downs of their team's fortunes to influence their joy in recent life, I took things to whole new levels. After bad losses I wouldn't just feel depressed, I would let it devour me, so much so that at one point I got into the habit of going to the Bears home ground and climbing the fence in the middle of the night so I could sit and look out on the field and relive every moment of a loss. Over time this developed to the point where North Sydney Oval became a place to break into to sit and summon up every drip of misery I could find until eventually, after years of trying, I could make myself cry. As time went by I developed numerous places to go and sit quietly and hate myself. Numerous remote waterfront locations with views of the city and remote parks joined my misery haunts, but North Sydney Oval was my favorite place to weep. I even missed my best friend Goshie's 21st birthday party so I could do this!

I don't do this anymore; at least not to the same crazy levels. However, my deep-rooted infatuation for self-sabotage continues to affect every part of my life. It's simple, really; if I hurt myself then other people can't get to me. If I fail because of something I do in advance, then it's not me that's rejected, it's this little failure that I can note and move on from. Really it's just pure stupidity, and can take the form of anything from being unable to leave my house for a class until I *know* I have to sprint to make it two minutes late, or sending out a book pitch that I'm know how has a spelling or grammar mistake. At the time I justify in my mind that I am testing people to see if they care more about me or nitpicking, but that's just in-the-moment convincing that disappears into its obvious foolishness the second I am judged on it, where I can berate my own idiocy, then comfortably think, 'At least that doesn't mean it's my work that sucks' and move on. It's a habit I didn't think I would ever be able to break, but thank Christ I am finally starting to recognize when I am about to self-sabotage and sometimes even stop myself!

To show one way I have begun to fight it, I will now tell you as romantic a tale as you can get from my life.

It was a late afternoon back when I was still in Los Angeles. I had yet to eat all day, because when I get caught up in writing I often don't eat at all until the evening. I also often eat so much during the day I don't get around to working. I am a man who does things to extremes. On this day I was feeling like eating something sweet, so I decided to head around to my favorite local diner and order up a plate of their delectable chocolate chip pancakes, and as I walked in the door, there she was.

It was an instant connection. She was the hostess, so her job was to seat me, and as I was eating alone, I assumed she would put me in one of their little behind-the-counter seats where they usually hide losers like me, but instead she put me in a seat facing directly towards her hostess station from where I could read my book in a 'read one sentence, eat one bite of food, gaze at her until I get caught, read one more sentence' manner.

She was gorgeous in a very quirky way, which is my bread and butter, and you better believe I love butter. I even wrote a song about it once.

I like butter
I like butter
Everything tastes better
With butter upon her
Unless the thing
You are buttering
Is itself a block of butter
In which case
YOU'RE JUST FUCKING WASTING IT
I MIGHT BE HAVING DINNER ROLLS TONIGHT
AND IF YOU EAT ALL THE BUTTER
THEY'LL BE TASTELESS
TASTELESS
TASTELESS
Tasteless
Tasteless...

She was a brunette with a slightly upturned nose and a mouth that could contort into a myriad of cute and sexy smiles and adorably animated thinking faces. And she wore a dress that showed off both her beauty and individual personality. I couldn't keep my eyes and mind off her. This was one of those moments where my mind just yelled 'this might be it!' It was lavid—beautiful, warm, wonderful, brilliant lavid.

She came over at one point to ask me how my pancakes were tasting, only to find that I had barely touched them and I suggested it was to prolong their enjoyment, and although they were undeniably delicious is was more to prolong my staring at her. However, now that she spoke to me she merely made something else clear to me; she had the voice of a four year old and I find that adorable, which makes me sound like a psycho, but I simply adore adorableness.

After exchanging numerous smiles throughout my slowly eaten meal, I paid up, timed my exit at a moment when she was liberated from work duties, and as I walked out we looked briefly into each other's eyes and I said 'goodbye' in a way I hoped conveyed 'I really want to see you again soon' and proceeded to let her dominate my thoughts for the next few hours.

I had class soon after that and the whole time I was there I was convincing myself I should go back to the same place for dinner just to see her again as soon as possible. Three mind-jumbled hours later and I exited class with haste, heading for dinner. There was someone I *needed* to see. It just could not wait. Only, something very weird happened as I reached the front door, a voice went off in my head:

'Hey Dave, you always do the creepy stalker thing when you get a crush on a girl, it never works, why not try something else this time?'

'Hmmm, um, what are talking about, David? I want to see her, this is where she works, what's the problem here?'

'You know what the problem is. You'll go in, she'll see you, she'll know that you were here three hours ago and that a return so quick must mean something, you won't have the balls to ask her out, so you'll just stare like a freak before awkwardly saying something weird to her on the way out, and then when she proceeds to always act scared when you come in from now on you'll remind yourself that it's not that she doesn't like you, but that you screwed up by rushing back to see her right away. Oh sure, you'll convince yourself that it's a better plan of attack to manipulate chance encounters, and hope over time 'fate' somehow takes over. (Sample repeating lyric from another song I once wrote: I don't believe in fate, that all you do is wait—got to love my self-crippling inconsistencies). You'll remind yourself that other times when you've pussied out have let you find out valuable deal breakers, like that she looks old enough but is actually fifteen, or has a boyfriend, or that one time you had lavid, followed the girl, and it turned out that she worked in a brothel (true story), then you'll beat yourself up, and hate yourself, and enter a new phase of prolonged loneliness. Or as I call it, you'll "go all Dave" on her!'

'Holy hell, this is that self-sabotage bullshit again, isn't it?'

'Um, um, um, um YOU THINK? My God, you're an idiot.'

I was right, and although I wanted to see her, I knew this was not the way to do this. I needed to be anywhere BUT stalking her. There was a comedy club around the corner that I frequented and performed at regularly, and I decided a good couple of hours of laughter might be just the thing to stop my mind racing with desire for this girl. And I don't mean sexual desire; this was lavid man, lavid!

I walk around the corner to the comedy club with a clear objective—have some laughs, hopefully run into some friends, and have enough beers that I won't have 'pining over cutie' insomnia ruining my next few days.

I was not expecting at all what transpired.

The girl... WAS IN THE SHOW!

It was an improv show and her job was to tell little anecdotes that would inspire improvisation. She even told a little story about how her dating life was completely messed up and that she mostly dated her customers from her job. Um, she was cute, messed up like me, she was practically saying out loud that 'I formed a crush on a customer today and that's inspired me to talk about how I DO date them, in case one of them was wondering', and my earlier last-second decision not to stalk her had instead planted me right at her feet.

Ah fate, just when I thought you were like original ideas coming out of modern hip-hop stars, i.e. comprehensibly non-existent, and here you are, not just real, but rolling in front of me laughing at your sweet practical joke of hiding before now.

I made sure as hell to talk to her as soon as I could after the show. Another sign that this wasn't just an infatuation because despite the fear I simply could not, *not* talk to her. I was boring as, but it's hard to be witty when your brain is screaming, 'THIS MAY BE THAT 'ONE' PEOPLE TALK ABOUT, DON'T FUCK IT UP, YOU KNOW, BY LETTING HER KNOW THAT YOU'RE THINKING THIS' and then she was torn from me by friends.

I ran home, and having heard her name announced on stage, I was able to facebook her. 'Don't stalk her, Dave, don't stalk her.'

Her photo had a picture of her with fast food mascot Jack, from 'Jack in the Box' and as a fast food addict this threw me over the top, and so I sent her a lame message about how it was nice to meet her, and I'd love to hang out with her sometime, 'if Jack doesn't mind'.

Within hours she had shot back that Jack would mind, because he was the jealous type. And after I had spent many hours wondering if this was her jumping in on a playful joke or a straight out shootdown, I attempted some sort of joke reply to her statement, and before I stopped checking my messages obsessively in hope of another silly reply, she changed her relationship status to 'in a relationship' and then started writing on her facebook wall about her new sex life with her new boyfriend.

Boo.

'Hey, fate?'

'Yeah, Dave?'

'You're a cunt!'

'Ha ha, I know.'

I got over it very swiftly. There is no way to make a girl seem less sexy than to attach her to a boyfriend and plant in my mind images of him having sex with her.

Later on, my lavid love let the world know through facebook that she was once again single, and at times she even suggested she was keen on finding a guy to spend time with in capacities other than friendship. My interest was rekindled, and I sent her a few creepy facebook messages and had the odd awkward conversation with her as I ran into her from time to time.

Of course, my time in America came to close and I returned to Australia sans love. I do think of this quirky cutie from time to time, though. And one day, late at night while I was trying to figure out another way to get a visa back to the states, I facebooked her this message:

'Will you marry me? I mean, it's not like I need a Greencard or anything.'

That may have been a mistake.

She did reply to let me know that her standards are high enough to still turn down facebook proposals. And I replied something like, 'That's the problem with you girls, your standards are too high.'

That may have been a mistake.

For some unknown reason, I doubt we will ever be together. She keeps me as a facebook friend for a very well-known reason; if there are weirdoes from a different country trying to marry you over facebook, it is easier to keep an eye on them if you stay friends.

Still, I did resist the urge to stalk her that first night, so I am officially learning! And really, everything is a good experience if you learn from it, right?

By the way, I wrote the first draft of this chapter on my phone on an exercise bike in my gym, and just as my time on the bike was up an absolute hottie came in. So I did what anyone would do, I extended my workout time. And despite several clear efforts to smile in her direction, she did NOT invite me back to her place, or smile back. She didn't even do that thing where girls tuck their shirts into their sports bras so you can check out their midriffs. I really don't know what I am doing wrong in this dating game.

Then I climbed into my elevator to head back to my apartment and as I turned to face the elevator mirror, I got an inkling. I had sweated so much that my white t-shirt was now see through, exposing very sweaty chest hair, and on either side was the drizzle of butter on the top of the meal—my nipples, standing out, standing up—as erect and pointy as they had ever been.

At least this one I didn't *self*-sabotage.

I AM AWFUL AT RELATIONSHIPS, SO TAKE SOME ADVICE FROM ME

Here are some things you should know, people.

GIRLS:

You say it over and over, and it's seemingly ALL of you—what is the number one thing you're looking for from a guy trying to get your attention? Confidence.

That is *RETARDED*!

Demanding a guy has confidence is like demanding someone enter Wimbledon and expecting him to have confidence that he's going to win the tournament. Ok, it's great if it's true he can win, but in this game, you girls are the tennis tournament and you better believe that this confidence, if present, comes from entering himself into plenty of other tournaments and that he's had a lot of success inside them. And there ain't no way he's going to build up this ability and not keep using it on as many tennis tournaments as he can. He's going to pound the hell out of every tournament he can get his sweaty paws on.

No, what you *want* is a guy that is just so happy and proud to be there, and just wants to enjoy and appreciate it as much as he can, because who knows if he'll ever get the chance to play again, so hell yeah he'll be nervous at his first press conference, and first match. Especially as he knows Mr. Confidence is out there, and almost always wins these things in the end. That's pressure, man! Give a non-manslut guy a break.

Actually, come to think of it, I should have used a golfing analogy, made a bunch of jokes about how quickly the most confident players know they can get in holes and then I could have merely said, 'Tiger Woods, I rest my case!'

But no, because I was a tennis prodigy for about two weeks when I was eight, and even I, having been one of probably only a couple of million people ever identified as having raw talent in tennis, even I having not picked up a racket in five years, would have no freaking confidence at all playing today! So yeah, Tiger Woods, I rest my case!

BOYS:

Celebrate all birthdays, anniversaries and special holidays 364 days early. It's perfect, you'll never forget another one, you'll always be the first to give a gift and you'll be considered fun, and quirky!

'I can't believe you forgot our anniversary again, you bastard!'

'Actually honey, I did not, and I can't believe you waited 363 days after I gave you a gift for you to give one to me!'

Reasons why this good:

- You get a warning every time
- Much easier to re-gift
- Day after sales
- If she is cheating on you and decides to tell you on the special day, it'll have been nearly a year since you gave her your gift, so the money you spent will seem a little less recently wasted
- Plus you probably don't have to give her your gift for next year anymore

- Unless you are kind of a pushover in which case, how the fuck did you get a girlfriend when I can't get one?

Yay, now everyone's happy! There you go—consider all relationship issues FIXED

I CAN'T HELP IT

I am useless at asking girls out. I am useless at being in relationships. I am useless at convincing girls they'd be happier right now if they were naked. I am useless at showing girls the best, sweetest, funniest, most endearing parts of myself. Yet more than anything, I am useless at break-ups.

I haven't had many relationships, yet there is one sure pattern that has developed upon each of them ending. Regardless of whether I considered her to be potentially the love of my life or whether I spent half my time with her mumbling to myself 'how the hell do I get out of this?' any break-up inevitably leads me to follow a familiar ten-step recovery process:

1. Get crushed in a way my body physically can barely handle. This will include crying, insomnia, excessive drinking, and physical self-harm with a garnish of astronomical self-loathing.
2. An attempt to share the wealth. Once I have descended into this hole I need to suck her into it. Unfortunately and disgracefully, this will usually take the form of e-mails and text messages designed as psychological bullets, crafted as metaphors and ambiguous predictions, where I pretend to myself that I am so smart she won't see through my obvious motives and will instead beat herself up the way I do to myself.

164

3. A period of intense 'knowledge' that I will be alone forever and the persistent pain that comes with realizing that.

4. A period of avoiding the very thought of the opposite sex manifesting itself over at least seven solid days by romanticizing the magic that is winter—I mean, how miraculous is it, you get all cold so you go into a restaurant and order soup. Once it comes, you.... *blow* on it.... to cool it down..... then you go back outside where you..... *blow* on your hands.... to *warm* them up! Wow! That's like the definition of magic.

5. Having reminded myself that the exceptionally unlikely can sometimes be a reality, I morph into a period of telling myself, 'I don't want love, I want endless filthy emotionless sex.'

6. Now it's time to hit on enough random girls to make it utterly clear that sex is not something I have any skill in acquiring, let alone endless filthy emotionless sex. Magic exists, my ass.

7. Now I like to write a series of 'jokes' from a happy optimistic part of my brain, for some reason mostly about AIDS.

Here are some of the most adorable examples:

- Proof life isn't fair; meet a girl with AIDS—bad luck! Meet a girl who won't put out—bad luck! That leaves seventeen girls out of three billion, tough odds.
- Make love not war. AIDS kills slower.
- Make love not war, worst slogan ever. First they tell the soldiers this and then they get upset when they start raping villagers. Make up your minds, assholes.
- Shocking news: If you have AIDS yet you're a virgin then there is a good chance you're horribly unlucky!
- I was mucking around with a chemistry set recently and I accidentally stumbled onto a cure for AIDS. I'm not telling anyone what it is, though, and you want to

know why? Well those AIDS victims are so unfriendly, they're often standoffish, hate to be touched or cuddled, and woe is me if you try to get one into bed! It's just sex, you prudes, it's not like you're virgins! They act like I have some sort of disease or something. I know they want me to help them out, but I'd rather find a dog that won't stop begging me for food and wipe peanut butter on my balls in front of it before taking a nap. I really am a well-balanced human.

8. Now I'm ready for a further period of self-loathing that includes numerous internal monologues about all the things I hate about women, usually centered around 'why do men have to do all the work when women have all the power of choice' and 'my God, when you're in a relationship every second girl you meet seems to make it clear she'd gladly take you off your girlfriend's hands, but then as soon as you are single they disappear, meaning most girls are boyfriend-stealing scum, meaning most girls are far too horrible as human beings to be even slightly datable, aaahhgggghhhhh!'

9. A realization that I need to be liked, touched, hugged, cared for, by just about any girl, 'please remind me I am lovable, PLEASE'!

10. The final step is finishing up with lots of time researching where I should move next after steps two, six, seven and nine have left me unable to show my face in pretty much any place in my current city.

The whole process is a rollercoaster ride of ups and downs that reminds you how wonderful life is. I recommend taking this on after *your* next break-up. In fact, if you're in a happy relationship at the moment I suggest you start pretending to receive mystery text messages so the doubt will build in your partner and you too can be dumped! It'll be worth it, trust me!

As for my latest journey down the ten-step program, it was during my prolonged stay in step nine that I really made an embarrassing atrocity of myself this year. Over the course of the past few years I have become more and more and more comfortable around the opposite sex. So much so that many, if not most, of my best friends, scattered around the world, are girls. I get along with them. I like who I am around them. I get to bring out my caring, loving side in their company. Plus, they are friends you get hugs from, and that's awesome.

This year I decided to ruin all this.

Like I said, I am useless at asking girls out, mostly because I am useless at reading the signs. I have *no idea* if a girl likes me or not, absolutely none. I read up about body language and study it in social situations. I people watch obsessively, always keenly focused on whether anyone is taking any notice of me whatsoever. And I listen for subtle or not-so-subtle things said that might suggest a girl I am talking to has some desire to see me again. Still I have no idea.

It was with all this in mind that this year I decided, at random points of phase nine, to read into things that did not exist and over the course of a couple of months burn just about every female friendship and acquaintance I had one-by-one by taking the pussy route by asking them all out via facebook messages, usually at 5am, and usually with incoherent alcohol ramblings or absurd half-awake, half in dreamland insomnia-sprawled lines of absurdity. I probably did this with twenty (ex) friends and about twenty more acquaintances, mostly girls who all hang out in the same two or three locations I spend most of my time too. Meaning, I am sure word of my quest got out, and I am sure conversations like this happened:

> 'Have you got one of David's crazy propositions yet?'
> 'Yeah, I got mine two weeks ago.'
> 'Oh really? Stefanie didn't get hers till last night!'
> 'Oh wow, I hope she is not upset at being number 39?'

'Of course not, she is proud it took so long. I mean, she knew it was going to happen, he has done it with everyone, but she likes not being the first to attract a crazy person.'

'Oh, I can imagine.'

'Did you reply to him when he asked you out?'

'No, no, we actually all got together early on and made a pact none of us ever would, that way it's *way* easier to make fun of him behind his back, and let's face it, right to his face!'

'Ha ha, what a humongous tool that guy is!'

'I know, if it wasn't so unendingly hilarious it may actually be a little sad.'

'Fortunately, it is simply so extraordinarily hilarious we don't even have to consider the sad side.'

'Right you are, right you are—ha ha ha ha!'

'Ha ha ha ha ha ha!'

'HA HA HA HA HA HA HA HA!'

'HA HA HA stop it, stop, it's, it's too funny, I'm choking, I'm choking, ha ha ha!'

Well the joke is on you ladies, while you were all making fun of me just because I did things wholeheartedly deserving of making fun of, I went out and figured out a simple four step program guaranteed to bring both fame and fortune, and because I, unlike possibly you, don't feel the need to hold grudges, I will now share it with you:

1. Start a sexual fetish
2. Attempt to sell it, and your body for it, for cash. Once you have failed at this (assuming you're a guy) you can then
3. Breed a kitten that coughs up money. Easy!

Or else:

4. Just write a series of hilarious AIDS jokes.

SWITCH OFF

Given some of my sexual confessions in this book so far, it may surprise you to hear that as a teenager and well into my early twenties, I was an absolute prude of the highest order. I was utterly positive I would only ever have sex with one person in my life and that I would be her only one too. If there were even a hint of a suggestion that a schoolmate I knew was already having sex, I'd write them off as a horribly immoral person. In fact, the thought of people still in high school having sex still bends my inner moral compass all the wrong ways. (Although, in all reality, it's more jealousy than prudishness now). I'm in my thirties and have never had regular sex and thirteen year olds get to? That's simply not fair. Whine, whine, whine.

When I got to about nineteen and reached the point of actually considering trying to get one of those girlfriend dealies, I started to write lists of pros and cons of girls I'd encounter in my world to try and decide if any of them were chaseable. On the 'pros' side of the list would often be this line:

She's not attractive and therefore more likely to be a virgin.

Yep. That is how sick I was about it. Let's break down this line a little more deeply. It can be interpreted in two ways, both true and both awful. One – it was such a deal breaker for me for a girl to have already had sex that I was willing to spend THE REST OF MY LIFE only EVER having sex with one girl, and to achieve this I was willing, or even desiring, for this to be a girl who *EVEN I* did not find even a little bit attractive. Two – I was so socially inept that I assumed that unattractiveness meant you WOULD BE a virgin. Like no less-than-perfect girl has ever offered up her body in the hope that offering more than other girls will get her some love.

I was so obsessed with virginity and mating for life with your first partner that I would not only not donate to AIDS charities but I would get mad at their very existence. 'There is already a cure for AIDS, you scumbags, it's called only ever having sex with your wife,' I'd rant in my head when someone shoved a white bin with a red ribbon painted on it in my face.

This was despite the fact that even then I found marriage an outright obtuse idea.

'I love you, honey, in fact I love you so much I have a question for you (gets down on one knee) will you, my love, permit me the pleasure of allowing the government and lawyers to now have a say in our relationship?'

'OH MY GOD! Of course, honey, ever since I was a little girl I have dreamed of having a relationship with a man and our elected officials, allowing their morals to play a part in my life whether I agree with them or not!'

These days I want to live and work in the United States of America but cannot, despite being financially secure, educated, speaking the language, passionate about what their country believes in, both politically and culturally, and also being kind of a nice guy who never really gets in trouble. Yet a non-English-speaking person, who openly hates America, has no intention of ever getting a job and paying taxes or learning local customs, or contributing to society in any way, and thinks stabbing someone in the face is ok as long as the cops don't find out, can get a Greencard simply by marrying someone?

I believe in complete equality of all people, but please don't let the gays get married. It is a stupid system that rates someone you met and married on the same night in Vegas over a friend you've had for decades. You don't expand stupid—you eradicate it!

I digress, where was I? Oh yeah, proving why no one should ever listen to my political ideals.

I was so virgin obsessed that I could not even form a minor crush without a weight of pain that someone else may have already banged her eating away at my drastically ill-equipped mental health.

Perhaps the most embarrassing consequence of this virgin obsession was this: the thought of a girl on a television show losing her virginity at only sixteen years old made me so mad for so long I put a stone cold boycott on one of my favorite TV shows.

'Claudia struggles to not lose her virginity' the TV guide read for what was to happen on this week's *Party of Five*. And yes, this being the show in question does nothing but make the fact I threw this TV guide at the wall in disgust and welled with fury all the more pathetic. I mean, I'd already allowed myself to forgive plenty of similar behavior on this very show, I was and am still scared by the love I had for the character Sarah (and the actress who played her – Jenifer Love Hewitt – stay tuned, my novella *Stuck In An Elevator With Jennifer Love Hewitt* will be released soon) on the show and I now denied myself her presence, despite pretty much every show I watched at that age having tons of sex with young people in them, and the fact I worshipped rock stars and football players who banged sixteen year olds like the world depended on it, but more than all that is that I allowed A FICTIONAL CHARACTER having sex to make me inconsolably upset!

Now a long time later, I have changed a lot. I am still kind of determined to make love to a virgin one day. Only now it's for a way more romantic reason—it is a beautiful gift that a girl can only ever give to one person and it would make me so happy to know that at least one girl on earth chose me. I mean, plenty of other bastards have had a crack at a hymen—I WANT MY BLOODY TURN!

Also, the young actress, Lacey Chabert, who played the guilty character, has now matured into one of the most stunningly beautiful girls on this planet. The only way I can truly overcome this memory is for me to now track her down and bang her. Wait, um, I mean, do something even slightly realistic. Date her? No, something she'd agree to. Meet me? Still probably not. How about this, I'll contact her management and tell them about this book

171

and tell them all I want to do is possibly meet Lacey, talk to her on the phone, maybe even Skype with her, or exchange emails, then when they get back to me and let me know which of those they have agreed to I will say to Lacey straight out something I should have said to her half a lifetime ago.

'Lacey, I no longer mind if fictional characters you play in your career lose their virginity.'

Despite her evocative beauty and a talent that thrived on television from a very young age, her career is not as successful as it should be. She should be one of the biggest stars in the world and she is not. Perhaps the fact no one like me has had the guts to say the above line to her is what has held her back?

So I contacted her management and her publicist and get this, they have NOT returned my emails yet! Are you not even looking out for your client, you bastards?

Stay tuned, more on this story hopefully to come. And I hope it doesn't lead to this:

'What's the purpose of your visit?' the US customs official say to me.

'I need to stalk actress Lacey Chabert until I get the opportunity to tell her I don't mind if her characters lose their virginity on TV anymore,' say I.

'(Talking into shoulder walkie-talkie) Prepare a jail cell and a straightjacket, please.'

The next show for me to boycott, only this time from the beginning, was a little show by the name of *Dawson's Creek*. I've seen about seven scenes of this show in my life, and every one had teenagers talking about sex the way only Rhodes Scholars who look like supermodels and have cured all STDs should. I downright hated this show and its very existence. There was no way I could watch it. The teenage sex was so in your face it made me feel sick to my jealous prudish stomach. I didn't just not watch it; I loathed it with a crazy zeal.

Years later, as mentioned earlier, I found myself at the Cannes Film Festival. One thing I did not mention before is that while there, I happened to fluke going to the premier of an incredible movie called *Blue Valentine*. And even more amazing was that the stars and producers, including God's gift to women Ryan Gosling, one of the most influential producers of all time Harvey Weinstein, and former star of the one and only *Dawson's Creek*, and now hugely respected multiple Oscar nominee Michelle Williams, all sat one row behind me to watch the film.

If you haven't already, go check out this film, it's sad and powerful, and beautifully acted, and on this particular screening, as the credits rolled the main players behind me were given a well deserved full ten-minute standing ovation and my friends and I were bang in the middle of it, right in the prime position to imagine for a few moments it was for us and feel that glow of being loved for doing what you love. It felt nothing short of marvelous.

As it ended, the clearly proud yet slightly embarrassed stars began to slowly make an adulation-bombarded departure, when something unexpected happened, and the gorgeous Michelle Williams and I locked eyes and shared a fleeting yet deep moment. It was weird, and beautiful, and probably all on my side. Her involvement in that creek-inspired sex show had long allowed me to be just the right kind of bitter to ignore her beauty, but in that moment I was engulfed by it.

After my failure with Lacey I thought about trying to locate one of the up-and-coming starlets to give them my permission to have sex in films, but more and more it occurred to me that this was just a fruitless effort. No one in Hollywood gives a shit that I was a prude. I am sure if I ran into one of these girls walking down the street and yelled, 'Hey, Dakota, it's ok with me if you lose your virginity in character in a movie,' it would be a memorable moment for them in some way. But it ain't going to happen.

Still, I am an often delusional man. What if Michelle and I really did share a moment? What if I sent her my story and it inspired her to at least Google me, see some pictures, perhaps remember me, or like some of my work? What if I could meet her? What if I could get to interview her and ask about that standing ovation and her subsequent Oscar nomination for the role? There are but a small handful of people who were right in the middle of that ovation—who else could offer to write about her Oscar experience from this angle? What if she met me and said, 'I remember that look, I have been thinking about you ever since, and I am so happy you have found me'? What if I could tell her I forgive her for *Dawson*, then lean in for a kiss and end up making love to her? What if we dated, and the media started to call me 'a poor replacement for Heath Ledger', her former partner and father of her daughter Matilda? What if the media pointed out I am yet another shaggy-haired Australian, just not one with the talent of Heath? What if this came to define my life? What if I could fucking just fantasize about a bloody celebrity without ruining it with my pathetically over imaginative sabotaging mind?

Seriously, I do this all the time. I hear women scream over someone like Matt Damon, and I think, 'You know he's married, right?' because if I even try to fantasize about a celebrity who I know to be in a relationship, it all breaks down in my mind. I have to split them up before I can even consider touching them with mental hands, and this sends me on fantastical paths of celebrity husband death, and I end up being a comforter, and that makes me feel bad for the dead dude, and I can't have imaginary sex while I am thinking of that stuff.

Still, I thought my angle of that ovation and her Oscar nomination might get me an interview with Michelle. In her management's defense, they did have the decency to email me back to tell me that I could not meet with Michelle but still wish me luck with my project, leaving me with nothing more than a whole pile of pathetic memories. And like a teenager who tries to slit her wrists as a cry for help more than a real suicide attempt, these memories of mine live on, unmurdered.

Anyway, I guess I'll just send it out to the world to all of you young starlets: I forgive you for the sex you've had or will have on TV. I'll even happily watch you lose your fictional virginities (while secretly hoping your real-life virginities are safely intact and we'll soon meet and after an incredibly adorable courtship bathed in sweetness you'll offer it to me). I'd like to tell you in person, well one or two of you in particular, but for some unfathomable reason your managers and publicists are not answering my emails.

And now a joke I used to tell that often got me in trouble: if someone does something to please you, you give then a pat on the back. Well I think if someone disappoints you, you should give them a pat on the front. And by the way, Dakota Fanning's movies disappoint me more and more the more she develops breasts.

FINGER LICKING GOOD
KISSING STORIES BY DAVE

Just in case any of the people mentioned or alluded to above do read this and choose to kiss me at some point, I should let you know I have developed into an awesome kisser. I have had many compliments in this department. And I am confident I can do the job with aplomb. Well, as long as I don't know it's coming up.

You see, just about every time in my life that I have been presented with the opportunity to properly make out with a girl I actually have genuine feelings for, right before I know that the next time I see her will be the time we really truly suck face together, I will develop a huge, ugly zit on the side of my mouth. Close enough to my mouth so that I can literally feel it sucking blood from my lips to fuel its continuing growth. At about the same time it has reached its full massive capacity, about the size of an eyeball, it will then develop a white head like a hot fudge sundae capped with puss instead of whipped cream. It doesn't matter how many times I pick this white head off in a bloody mess, for at least two days it will grow back like the liquid terminator in *Terminator 2*. I swear I can watch it grow.

I have deep horrendous memories of the first time I ever properly made out with a girl. It was at night on a beach. It was windy yet warm, and the moonlight and the crashing waves made it quite a romantic setting. And I had an alien growing out of the

176

side of my face, which throbbed like a penis after living in a strip club for a month and not being allowed to jerk off the whole time. Still, I went for the kissing. After all, I was now officially days into my twenties and I had never *made out* with anyone and I was going to go for this despite it being the least sexy situation of all time.

Now, let's just be clear: when you have a zit the size of a ruby-red grapefruit hanging off the fringe of your lip, and a zit which is raw and full of life and feeling, and you have two inexperienced practitioners of the fine art of French kissing, especially when both are most likely equally repulsed by each other as they are attracted, well the zit gets a lot of attention from your partner's tongue.

I could feel a combination of sting and relief every time she lacquered my pimple with her saliva. Almost like the application of aloe to a fresh red-raw sunburnt back, it felt at once soothing, painful, tender, and utterly disgusting. I felt for her, I felt for myself, and then she swiped her tongue across this mountain like a condor sweeping to ground to take a helpless field mouse into its mighty beak, and I was positive immediately that she had just removed the white head once more, and I could feel this cunt of thing oozing puss which she seemed to lick up gleefully, I guess, assuming the wetness was but the combination of our sloppy unrefined kissing. My mind has now morphed this entire memory into a cartoon where we become Tim Burtonesque monsters that engulf each other in vulgarity, with our faces literally melting into the others. Although at the time it was clearly the best moment of my life.

To this day I still get these malicious zits and almost always right at a time I know my mouth might finally be copping some attention in some way or another.

These particular side-of-mouth pimples really are the worst. If you just bleed them out, they grow back big and strong the following day. They hurt more than anything else your body decided to spontaneously grow at any time or another. They are the one place to get a pimple that results in people staring with disgust. Grow the same thing on the back of your neck and people will be grossed out, but they don't question whether your lifelong friendship is worth saving in order to put up with seeing this thing for the next few weeks.

And this is the real thing; they are survivors! Any other pimple on your face you can pretty much dry out, pick off and be done with all but a few days after they first sprout. Not these things. They hang around for weeks. And then even when they finally die, it's a slow death. And then even as they waddle away like a log of dog shit dumped on a sidewalk in a rain storm, they grow coarse, and harden, which means opening your mouth often creates a tear in skin, and forces you to eat dinner with one napkin used primarily for mopping up blood after every large bite. Then to confound the problem even more, the constant reopening of this evil wound creates a red scar that can sometimes take months to heal, and in the meantime make you look like you have herpes growing on your lip. At least when it was ten times as big in the prime of its life, the white head reminded people it was merely a pimple, and not an incurable disease they can catch if too close to your face.

I hate these scumbags. I still often grow in some resemblance of a moustache and beard with the intended purpose to cover up the current or left-over remembrance of this plague of my face. And if for one reason or another I find myself having to shave clean, it is almost unheard of for the side of my mouth not to cunt me over once more with a hastily grown zit that blooms with a speed mocking that of my bearded disguise.

Oh, the joyful life.

The second girl I ever made out with got there a couple of days before the development of a zit the size of a basketball on my lip. It was brewing when we kissed, I could feel my skin pulsate and sting, and the next day it exploded. A few days after that this girl's poor grandmother died, and the night of the funeral she wanted me to come to the wake and comfort her. I was in a state of not needing to be seen by anyone for at least a few days, and especially not her whole family and many of her friends who would be meeting me for the first time, and none of whom would be in the mood for thinking about things truly sickening. But when a girl you're hoping to be your girlfriend asks you to come to the wake for her dead grandmother, you go, right? You can't possibly say no. Especially when on the phone she is sweet and needy in a way you're sure has made the courtship fast-forward in a way only a death could achieve.

People looked at me that night like I was a leper with an open wound on my face, when only the second part of that is true. While this girl did eventually agree to go out with me again, over a month later (then take my virginity, see opening chapter), she never once admitted to any friends or family we were dating, a pattern which would come up in my life several more times. However, at one point during this wake she fell asleep as we watched a movie together (anything to not look at me) and while she slept I touched her boobs. Was that wrong of me?

How do you murder memories like this? Well, I did it by winning an Oscar—hell yeah!

It was my Birthday eve and in forty minutes the clock would strike midnight and birth me a new age and I was getting lots of hugs and kisses from my female friends. Then a male friend, a big sweaty English geezer named Oscar, was feeling left out, so he gave me a kiss on the cheek, then whipped a bit closer and planted one on my mouth. The girls saw and urged photographic proof it had happened, and because I am an absolute whore for making people laugh, I offered to let him kiss me again, and as I puckered up, with eyes closed because I am so romantic, he slipped the tongue deep in. Thanks, mate, I have officially tongue kissed a man (and yes the photographic proof is online).

Then a couple of hours later, after we had gotten wasted in no small way, the fault of the club, because this place plays this one awful song numerous times a night, and we have a new drinking game where we have to drink a shot of tequila every time they do, and they played it many times, so I got kicked out for standing talking to my friend, then some cops tried to agitate me in the hope I'd start a fight, so they could hit me with their nightsticks and keep whining to the media that Sydney drunks are out of control with violence and get more revenue. It's kind of like AIDS researchers going out and stabbing children in the eyes with AIDS needles so they can say, 'Now kids are getting it—give us more research money!'

But the point is, I have gone from a man with a mouth so gross that only a couple of clearly deranged girls would go near it, to a man who attracts the tongues of both sexes—that means *everyone* wants to kiss me. And the memory of my worst ever tongue kiss, my first ever tongue kiss, has now been replaced with an even worse tongue kiss. Get this noose around your neck, you dirty memory!

By the way, no offense Oscar, but kissing a guy is horrible! Seriously, I now know why I find it so hard to pick up girls; guys' mouths are gross, their tongues are big and obtrusive and those beard whiskers are horrible. Honestly, girls, go lesbian, kissing a girl is much better, trust me; just watch out for zits. But if you do want to kiss a guy, I have good news, I recently acquired Dr Pepper flavored lip balm, so instead of blood and puss, my lips now taste of sweet soda, see, I told you I was a good kisser!

TRIPPING DOWN THE TRADITIONAL

As you may have noticed, my severely late puberty has been a source of pain for me. In reality, my young nature has been there as long as I remember. I don't really have any memories of it but apparently my lack of aging or growing was a concern for my family when I was younger and doctors thought I'd be very lucky if I ever reached an adult height.

I recall being around fifteen or sixteen and just praying I would one day reach 5'3", the height of Mugsy Bogues, the shortest player ever to play basketball in the NBA. In a rare sign of self-confidence in my brief basketball-obsessed years, I was sure that if I could reach his height I could follow him into the NBA. Incredibly, at around my seventeenth birthday when I was still a ways from reaching this height goal, I went to an NBA game to see the Golden State Warriors play the San Antonio Spurs and I recall thinking I could hold my own if my fat ass was thrown on even then. Travel has always brought out my happy, optimistic and deluded sides.

I have no idea how I got to 5'10" or when I reached there, but it shocked everyone, although it didn't change how young I look. People now say over and over that I'm lucky now that I look so young, and damn right I am. I still get asked for ID every time I go out, even in Australia where I'm nearly sixteen years past the legal age. In two years I'll be double it and I know I will still get

IDed constantly, and I enjoy it every time, especially when I'm with people much younger than me who don't get asked. It's a nice change from when I was in my early twenties and numerous times my ID was photocopied and faxed to the police station because although bouncers and bar staff couldn't find any flaws in my driver's license, they still didn't believe it was me, or real.

I still enjoy letting people get to know me before they discover my real age; it's always a joy when they get a shock. Yet, right there in that lovely compliment is the root of a long-lived problem. When I was nineteen I looked eleven and the only girls even borderline attracted to me were ten. That's not fun. Now that I'm thirty-three I look about twenty-four or twenty-five and the eighteen to twenty-four year olds that I attract are freaked out by the age difference.

Two true stories:

1. I met my second girlfriend when I was twenty and she was sixteen. When we exchanged our ages upon our meeting, she was very reluctant to tell hers first. As she told me later, she was going to tell me that she was fourteen because she thought I was probably no older than fifteen, then she decided to just tell the truth because if I turned out that young she didn't want to know me anyway.
2. My third girlfriend was when I was thirty and she was eighteen. We decided she'd lie and tell her friends and family that I was twenty-four and they all freaked out that she was dating someone as old as twenty-four!

I basically meet two age groups of girls. Ones that I look close in age to, who think I am too old for them, and ones that are closer to my age and are looking for a far more mature man than me, preferably one that wants to settle down (I refuse to 'settle' for anything, especially something as negative as 'down'), and really, no one picks someone as unstable as me to settle down with anyway.

I don't like this. I am not a thirty-three year old. I just am not. Literally, the only thing about me that's thirty-three is my birth certificate. I don't look it, I don't act it, I don't feel it, I don't live like it, I don't smell like it, I even tie ribbons like a younger man (i.e. not at all)!

Those of us in the Western world have been stuck using this outdated ancient birth certificate method to determine our age for far too long. Our age determines so much about us, from what we are legally allowed to do, to how much we pay for amusement parks, to whether or not society forgives us for passing out drunk on someone's lawn. And we have absolutely no influence or sway in how we answer the question 'how old are you?' We're only allowed to use the birth certificate. That's downright nuts. More than that, sometimes we have to sit and cop people saying, 'Aren't you too old for this?' How dare you?

Well, as someone who wishes to change his legal and social age in a way that is widely recognized and respected, I have instead asked the ISSS (International Society of Scientists who like Superness) to come up with a brief and simple questionnaire to determine your actual age and demand that your actual age be changed on your passport and driver's license as often as you renew them at the very minimum.

Here is how it works: You fill out the scientifically formulated ten questions below, and average out your age, then that's your actual age. I will put in my answers to demonstrate.

1. How old do you look? 24
2. How old do you act? 24
3. How old do people guess you are? 24
4. You meet a girl you find really cute and she tells you she is 18, how old do you tell her you are? 24
5. It's been 14 years since you grew your first pube, how old should that make you? 24
6. How many years will it be before you get your first kiss without at least one zit on your face? 24
7. How many times do you masturbate for every time you have sex? 2,400,000

8. How many hours in a day are you the age you think you are? 24
9. If you buy a bag of cashews and there are 24 cashews in the bag how many would you eat if you were really hungry and enjoyed consuming cashews? 24
10. What's your favorite brand of bagged snow? 24

Now to do the simple math

24+24+24+24+24+24+2,400,000+24+24+24

= 2,400,216

2,400,216/10 = 240,021.6

So having crunched the numbers my *real* age would be 240,021 and six days old!

Wait, what the fuck? That is fucking outrageous! That means my birthday was six days ago and I fucking missed it, this is utter bullshit. Screw you, ISSS. I totally thought this thing was supposed to make me out to be 24!

Screw it; I want to be 24, so I'm just going to be 24. I have been saying I'm going to do this for years but it's my birthday *this* week, not 6 days ago, you bastards. It's time. I'm going to officially change my age back 10 years. This year, my 34th birthday will be celebrated, as my 24th and I will live as such from now on. Some may call me a liar but I say I'm finally telling the truth.

Silliness aside, I have many times over the past few years thought I will just literally start being ten years younger. It's easy to do the math, so the lie will be easy to maintain, and it's not like anyone will challenge me, because it's the age people guess I am.

I live with this plan in my heart for a day or so and it feels brilliant. It's a huge weight off my shoulders. Suddenly I am right where I should be at this age. I am passionate about my career but still learning and not in a rush to 'make it'. My relationship history is dirt, but I'm still young and in the experimental stage. If I get drunk and pass out on someone's lawn and they wake me up with a hose, I'll yell, 'I'm 24!' and they will merely say, 'Run on home, you scallywag!' It makes perfect sense.

Then I imagine meeting a girl I really like, we fall for each other, and then I tell her I've been lying about my age, and I'm not 6 years older than her but 16, and then she pukes on my chest, knees me in the balls and adds me to every sexual predator website known to man, which all makes me think I don't want to lie.

So, it was my birthday, and I figured why not suck on this little cyanide pill of a memory and at least experience taking ten years off before I discard it forever? So I celebrated my birthday like it was my 24th in all its 24th glory. I posted all over the internet, 'Yay, I'm 24 today', I went out partying with a bunch of friends who all referred to it as my 24th (and a couple of new people in my life who thought it actually *was* my 24th), I wore a birthday cake-shaped top hat and had songs requested for my birthday (which they wouldn't play, bastards) and yelled out 'IT'S MY BIRTHDAY' over and over so everyone would know for sure it was my birthday, and when they asked me how old I was I yelled, 'TWENTY-FOUR TODAY!'

How did people react? Not one person doubted me for one single second (single being redundant or else I would have used the plural 'seconds'). At one point a girl came up to me and said, 'It's my birthday too, only I'm thirty today,' then she nearly burst into tears and continued, 'I wish I was still young like you.'

Hell freaking yeah. I am not a liar. I hate lying and I hate people lying to me, but this was truth in a whole new fashion. Plus, for the first birthday in years I wasn't the one crying that I wished I were younger. And as a 24 year old I am now the perfect age to start my rookie season in the NBA—call me, Golden State Warriors!

ALL THE INFORMATION YOU NEED IS IN THE GUEST DIRECTORY

I have opened up a weird door in my soul and my brain this year. It turns out that the mind hides these embarrassing memories for a downright good reason, to protect you from them. Well, I have let out the beast and with the gates opening wider and wider, the spirits are coming faster and faster, and I'm trying to shoot them all down, but I am getting overwhelmed.

By the way, consider these sobering thoughts:

- I read a survey recently about the sexual habits of Australians, and under the heading 'when did you lose your virginity?' 8% ticked the box 'Ages 11-12'. Are you fucking kidding me? By which I mean, that's kids fucking and that simply is not right!
- A couple of days later I was in the passenger seat of a car and the warning label for the airbag claimed that it was not safe for children aged twelve and younger to sit in the front seat. That means in all possibility there are parents out there who have their kids say to them, 'Mum, can I sit up front?' and the parents can say, 'Look,

it's not safe, ok, why don't you go back to fucking your little friend back there!'

- Also, one day a man (probably) was in a board meeting at the clothing company he worked at and when the big bosses asked, 'Has anyone got any ideas for new product lines?' he cleared his voice, and hopefully with at least a tinge of doubt, said, 'What if we start marketing g-strings and other lingerie to pre-teen girls?' And not only was he not arrested, but this marked the beginning of a thriving merchandise wing of all department stores.

Now, the point should be that these are signs of a world gone mad, but maybe it's just me who is mad. Consider this selection of other thoughts and facts about me that I simply can't begin to think how to fix:

- I can't sleep without something to cuddle, with my two favorite options, girls and cats, rarely available to me, I usually go with a pillow, but anytime I have to share a room with a man I panic they will wake up to find me sleepwalk cuddling them.
- Rather than asking out a girl I had just met, who worked in the store adjacent to my home, I once wrote a blog about how I wished I'd asked her out, then went and told her that I wrote a blog and she should check it out and wrote down the address for her. She always looked at me funny after that.
- I once suspected a girlfriend of cheating on me so I went to spy on her over a fence, and I got to see firsthand evidence that she was, then someone called the cops on me.
- There are like three-hundred awful girlfriend stories in this book, but I have only had four girlfriends, and three of them lasted less than six weeks; how the hell do I fit so much pain into such short periods?

- I can fly in most of my dreams and panic I'll one day sleepwalk off my balcony, yet I regularly decide the risk is worth the view.
- I believe I can one day have a long-term relationship where we never have a single fight.
- If I meet you and I'm not the NEXT person you kiss, I NEVER want to kiss you. This does not lead to many kisses.
- I am adamant you should only be allowed to get mad at people for doing things you've NEVER done, and I'm frequently pissed off at people for breaking this rule.
- I can't walk past a person holding up an umbrella without picturing one of its spokes gouging out my eyeballs. On really rainy days in busy cities I can picture hundreds of eye gouges an hour.
- If there is food on my plate at the end of a meal, it's either something gross (like a vegetable) or I'm dead.
- I'm habitually sexually attracted to mannequins.
- It gets worse—I even bought a mannequin, and yes I have fondled and cuddled her many times. I've never named her, but for a while I gave her a photocopy face of Elisha Cuthbert.
- I am desperately afraid of making phone calls yet I once placed a pathetic classified advertisement over the phone looking for groupies for my band that never even played a gig.
- I'm obsessed with the fly on my pants. I'm always playing with it, especially after just washing my hands after the bathroom and I often leave just-washed-hands wet patches there, plus I often leave actual urine wet patches there, and not that infrequently the wet patches are my excessive pre-cum stains. Which is it today? Who the hell knows?
- I get laid so infrequently that sometimes when I take a big shit I literally blow a load. Not an orgasm, just my body getting rid of stuff it knows I have no use for.

As I returned to Australia, my plan was to get back to work and show all my countrymen how I have grown and all that I have learned in my time away. Truth is, I've done none of it. I have been treating my body like a bloody trash can. I've eaten and drunk so much I am officially too fat for my belt. I did a three-day juice detox right after my birthday and lost a pile of weight and was still too fat to get my belt back on, and then went right back to eating and drinking like shit. On New Year's Day my party folk and I ate Pizza Hut for breakfast, McDonald's for lunch and KFC for dinner; this is not unusual for me.

I should point out that despite being a fast food addict, and being adamant that it benefits my life more than it takes away from it, one of the worst things that ever happened to me was because of McDonald's. I had snuck off from School Chapel to go to Maccas with some friends. I had been doing this daily for ages, but this time we were caught. We were all sentenced to Saturday detentions. And while studying on this fateful day I did something that at the time I found wonderful—I finally figured out the economic multiplier theory!

I know—exciting, right?

This was a key economic principle that made up a significant part of our final exams and having finally figured it out I now passed economics well enough to qualify to study for a degree in it, leading to three and a half years of boredom and misery at university, followed by using that degree to secure boring and miserable jobs in finance. All up, that fucking Quarter Pounder cost me ten years of my life!

You'd think I learn, but instead I treat my body like a literal trash can.

Truth is, at this point of my memory murdering adventure; I am in a bit of a hole. Clearly I am taking a humorous bent in how I present many of these stories from my life, but on the serious side, I really had planned to do some severe repair work on my psyche. And I have, sort of, but I thought I would be done by now, and I am not even close.

I honestly thought that my cancer charity would be a big success and end up being a huge part of this story. I felt the same about my acts of niceness adventure. And both went belly up before they started. But I keep trying to think up ways to change the world. So I can't get you people to do or say something nice, well, how about a holiday? Some people say there are too many already but that's simply not true—you can't have too much fun, and holidays are all about fun! Well, apart from Valentine's Day, of course, which is about romancing your loved one on the anniversary of when all the guys she banged before you did it to her before you. Aren't anniversaries sweet? By the way, little known fact: When St Valentine headed up to heaven, God thought he was such a likable lad that he sent him on a mission to hell for one last try at getting Satan to return to the flock and while down there Satan had him raped by a demon. Saint V enjoyed this so much that upon his return to heaven he sent orders to start a holiday based around love, and begged God to let his demon lover have another crack at being human so he could earn his place in heaven and he and Valentine could be together. God reluctantly agreed and the demon was sent into the body of a newborn in Austria where he was christened Adolf. So yeah, if you like the rape of angels and Hitler, go ahead and celebrate Valentine's Day all that you want! Or why not celebrate these holidays that I have invented? World World Day: where everyone in the world celebrates the rest of the world. Seriously, patriotism is great but so are countries other than yours, give them a chance. I suggest feasting on foods brought to your country by foreigners, or watching movies from elsewhere, or masturbating to ethnic porn.

World Losing Our Virginity Day: where everyone must do something for the first time. I suggest something adrenalin pumping, or self-improving, or if you have teenagers, finding new ways to chain them to stuff.

World Stop Being An Asshole Day: I see assholes out and about all the time. If I had to live like one of them I would so need a day off at least once a year, so take a day off, and I don't know, maybe swing past my website and say something nice?

Why am I so obsessed with trying to change the world when this year was supposed to be dedicated to self-improvement? I really need to start taking better care of myself. I need to get back on track and get back to making myself who I need to be. You know what, I'm going to do it too. In actual fact, I'm off to McDonald's right now to write up a plan.

IT WAS THE HEAT OF
THE MOMENT

A number of years ago I saw a girl at my local newsagent and I formed an instant crush. Lavid at its best and brightest. For a good year or two I made a point to buy my daily newspaper at her shop as often as possible and every time she turned out to be working there, I melted into a mess while convincing myself that she was *not* blushing, because if I believed she was then that would mean I would have to make a move and risk being rejected. You know, better to avoid pain than chase happiness.

It was one of those innocent infatuations where you know it won't go anywhere yet it was nice to think about.

Then one day I was sitting in a park eating my lunch and she suddenly appeared and sat down near me. I summoned up every ounce of guts in my entire body and about twelve minutes later let out a muffled airy, 'Hi.'

I honestly don't remember what we talked about, but it was easy, and sweet and nerve-racking, and I left with her phone number. Later that night I broke every rule in the book and texted her to tell her I had a big crush on her. She responded immediately, reciprocating.

We went to a movie a day later, and fell for each other hard. I hadn't had a girlfriend in over a decade and I suddenly knew what all those couple-type people were always so happy about. We'd meet for breakfast and even if we both had other plans we would keep coming back to see each other, sometimes four or five times a day, and to sound corny for a minute, it was magical.

Then, well you may know the drill by now, right as I was sure this might actually be something very significant, she cheated on me and dumped me for another guy. (This is the girl from the alcoholism chapter.)

I have often wondered what would have happened if I had made a move earlier. Actually, I know what would have happened. I would have asked her out, and then she would have told me she was only seventeen, and I would have gone to jail. Eighteen— magical, seventeen—criminal. Have I mentioned yet that I'm still deathly jealous of people who experienced romance and sex in their teens.

Still, the real lesson is that for most of my life spontaneity was like a deadly snake; to be avoided unless I had a huge blister I was too scared to pop on my own.

These days I tell people over and over that I live about as spontaneously as a human can. That is why when my friend Terry recently invited me at the last minute to go skiing with him in Canada, I said no right away. Then I changed my mind to maybe. Then back to no. Then hell yeah. Then, well, I really can't. But then, after a lot more thought I decided that if I could get some things organized I could maybe think about it. Why pass these things up?

And you know what? I'm a fool. What have I been doing with my life? I am writing the first version of this chapter right now while standing on my skis typing into my phone on top of a mountain out in the stunningly beautiful Whistler, British Columbia, Canada!

This was so not the plan for what was coming up, but, hey, it was Whistler—you get the chance to go and you go. And I was having enormous fun—I was getting exercise, I was soaking up the splendor, and was getting back into my long-forgotten lost love— adventure! I've spent so much time recently basically doing nothing and passing this bullshit existence off as research for my writing. Yet LIVING life is what I need to do. And living it healthily.

Sure, on this trip I also had to skip my dreamed-of heli-ski because of a horrible issue I will talk about shortly, and I also got so drunk one night that apparently I went streaking in the snow without even the slightest recollection of it, and also made my semi-monthly Twitter fool of myself.

Below is an example of some tweets one night. I've left the spelling mistakes in, and my point is lost even on me:

- The good thing about prick tease gold diggers is how they use up your generosity so if u ever meet someone who genuinely likes u cunt them
- Wow, If you're a girl & u like cunts you'd have ur pick of guys, also if you like rich good heated sweethearts but we all know u prefer cunts
- The point of vagina Is vagina & yet gash gash gash, fuck u u realistic cunt ect predgucipe ect

But I also got up early most days for the first time in years, and had fresh snow under blue skies, and the day after my nudie run I even did a forty-five minute uphill snow hike to ski the type of snow so good you have to EARN it.

I'm sick of my bullshit existence, the real Dave is back, baby! Now I want to buy a paper, not for the news, or the potential for statutory rape, but for the shear spontaneity of it.

Update: It turned out by keeping my data roaming on while I was overseas those tweets above cost me nearly as much as the trip to Whistler, nothing to be angry about today!

IF I COULD ONLY
DO ONE THING

I used to eat dirt a lot when I was a kid. That's probably not something completely unusual; kids do weird things to impress other kids. But here is why it was particularly weird for me—I did it not to impress other kids but just for my own pleasure. I used to get a cheese and lettuce sandwich every day and I took a weird pleasure in figuring out how much dirt I could get in there and still be able to eat it. I don't know why, I guess I have always liked a challenge.

I also hated to poo when I was a kid. (By the way, my brand new Microsoft Word spell-check doesn't recognize the word poo but my two–year-old nephew does. I guess there is a reason Microsoft-based computers and the politically correct movement both call themselves PC—in protest I am now going to take a small internet porn break, just to cleanse myself of this bullshit.)

La da da, la la, da, duh duh duh (please hear in your head time-wasting music rather than porn music, unless you too take a porn break, and if so, good for you, I like anyone who takes action against unnecessary censorship.)

(Wait, I was going to quit watching porn this year, maybe I can go back and delete that promise and no one will know... done, phew)

Ok, I'm back. Where was I? Oh yeah, I used to hate to shit (are you happy Microsoft, you're obtrusive squiggly red line has forced me to swear instead). I don't know why this was, because from memory I had a flawless diet, but for some reason I found it painful. So I held it, and the longer you hold it the more it ends up hurting, so I found myself spiraling into a pattern where I would regularly go weeks on end without shitting, by which time it would hurt so much the memory would make me never want to ever do it again, and so the pattern would repeat.

Because of this I often left 'deposits' in my underwear (sometimes BIG, round, bouncy deposits that I'd throw at things—did you need to hear that?) One time this saw me wiping my ass beside a massive highway with a huge leaf. And once my mother found out what was going on, I was often forced to undergo random underwear checks at various times and if 'deposits' were found I would get in trouble.

So, it was my birthday and we were having a party. I had been told I didn't get to have any of my own cake unless I passed the underwear test, and I failed badly, or messily or whatever (underwear checks aren't judged on a usual marking curve!), so no cake for me, on my own fucking birthday.

I was hurt, and embarrassed, so it was time to fight back. Yeah, that's right, in front of all my friends and well wishers sitting at the dining table, I screamed, 'It's my BIRTHDAY!' before releasing a myriad of tears, followed by digging into an adjacent garden and shoveling dirt into my mouth like an African villager at a Vegas Buffet. Take THAT! (It only just occurred to me as I am writing this that this is also the garden our cat used to spend its own private time failing the underwear test—revenge is never pretty).

My family still eats Christmas lunch at this same table every year, and every year I can't help but look across to where the dirt came from, and horribly imagining it in my mouth. These days crazy imagination remains strong, but the thought of anything granule-like in my mouth is now utterly disgusting.

I still have an outright despicable diet. I actually feel healthier when I eat junk. Vegetables make me feel nauseous. And if I wasn't constantly going on harsh diets, and slaughtering myself at the gym, I would quickly return to my teenage state of the common household enormous obesetoid.

On the other hand, food is great. A great meal can make you feel great, hence the term 'great' meal. Food tastes good, brings people together, and even tastes good. And good is good, just like good food tastes good, sometimes even great!

In fact, sometimes it's worth going halfway around the world for.

Despite what you may be hearing from this little tale of my life, at heart I am nothing short of a hopeless romantic. At least several times a week, if not several times a day, I will go off on mental flights of fantasy, dreaming of making a new life with someone new, a new career path, and quite often new cities, where I would re-invent my career, and meet someone new.

I love the dream of the unknown. *Known* is an uninspiring ball suck. When I am travelling and something goes wrong, reservations lost, flights missed, while my travel companions panic and/or get angry and frustrated, I try to stop letting them know what absolute glee I am feeling. We don't know what we're going to do, or where we're going to end up? Hello mind, enjoy fantasizing about all the possibilities.

For some reason Portland, Oregon is a city that has long been part of my fantasies as a potential place to re-invent my life. I don't know why, other than that I've heard it's full of misfits, and artists, and weirdoes, and quirky awesome people, and so clearly may be a place I may possibly fit right in. Having reached British Columbia to ski, I could not not head down the mere few hundred miles to see this great city. I promised I was getting back into being a spontaneous adventurous self, didn't I? I have to actually follow up on *some* of these pledges.

So, did the romantic dream of a new home come true? How the hell would I know, I wasn't here for that, I was here to study voodoo.

I have stuck some weird things in my body and it was time to do weird eating the right way— at Voodoo Donuts. When the proverbial 'if you could only ever eat one more thing' question comes up, I blurt out 'DONUTS!' then wipe a mouthful of drool out of my beard, and then I burst into tears because that means I'll never eat bacon again. 'No more bacon? SNIFF But you may be my best friend ever, SNIFF I swear SNIFF, I will never ever forget you SNIFF, or replace you with another SNIFF?' (RO-RO-RO-ROMANTIC!).

So I woke up after my best night's sleep in about seventeen years, with a crook neck, moaning, 'Why does my body hate me so?' then walk around in the cold consistent dreary rain for about an hour in the old town/homeless area (still really 'old-school America' beautiful), getting drenched in my brand new, expensive yet ugly and uncomfortable jeans (you're dead to me Levi) that I bought because I was getting too fat for my old ones, and just as I was about to give up on finding it, there it was, the famous, tiny, wonderful Voodoo Donuts.

I was greeted by a cute girl in a rainbow tie-dye shirt who immediately picked my accent and raved how much she loved how Australians love to travel (the weird thing is I have been feeling unpatriotic due to my desire to spend so much time away from Australia, forgetting that this is one of the very things I too love about Australians).

Two minutes later I had done something downright monumental, I purchased a cream cheese peach fritter the size of my head, having been distracted by the seven million colorful sprinkles, an Oreo donut, and most importantly - a maple-flavored donut, with BACON on it! A BACON DONUT! No more tears for me if I have to choose one more food product, now it's time to race back to the warmth of my room to get lost in gluttony!

So, how was it? Well, I must admit I was still pretty nervous about the prospect of bacon on a donut, no matter how long it has been since I have coveted one, so how was it?

HOLY HELL THIS SHIT IS AWESOME! Bacon, on a donut, is BRILLIANT!

I DEMAND Voodoo become a worldwide chain within weeks. Hey greenies, put down your anti-global warming machines immediately, there is a bigger problem facing the world: Most people, MOST people, still don't have access to bacon on donuts. This *must* be fixed immediately!

Oh yeah, let's back up to that romantic notion again for a moment. Did Portland fulfill the dream? Are you not paying attention? BACON ON DONUTS! But in all seriousness, no it didn't, not really. It's a great and beautiful city, and in twenty-four hours I met some really friendly people, but I didn't feel that positive vibe or gut feeling I was looking for (and Dewy has been on fire recently). Then again, I did arrive here, alone, after getting up at 5:15 am to travel on Greyhound buses for nine hours, on the most miserable day of the year—Valentine's Day.

AND NOW RANDOM VALENTINE'S DAY THOUGHTS By DAVE:

- It's official; tomorrow will be my first Valentine's Day ever waking up with a second human in the room. I hope my mate Nate at least attempts to grow a vagina tonight
- My Valentine today is a big long fat steel vibrating while thrusting forward Greyhound bus!
- Didn't expect this prolonged human touch today, then again I didn't expect a 400lb man to sit next to me on the bus; the toothless mulletted weird skinny guys are a more likely bet
- Now time to eat alone in a strange city on Valentine's— can't wait to see all of those horny couples' miserably jealous faces. Woo ha ha!
- It's 8pm on Valentine's Day and not a single soul in downtown Portland McDonald's, yet I'm the one who can't get a girlfriend? Lift your game, Portland boys!
- Really strange observation of the night—all the stereotypically attractive people out walking are hand in hand with a similarly stereotypically attractive member of the opposite sex, yet all the uglies are wandering somberly alone. Was there a memo I didn't get?

- For the first and only possible time in my life, I have spent 34 Valentine's Days in a row alone. Wait, um.... if I live to 68 I could comfortably do that again. I'll take bets starting at $5 that I can pull the repeat!
- When did I become such a gambling whore?
- I'm such a romantic I'm going to go eat dirt

A SPANISH OUTPOURING

Travel and food are definitely two things known to bring me joy. While on our backpacking journey around Europe, Goshie and I found ourselves in the beautiful seaside town of San Sebastian, Spain. It was around two days since we had been in Paris and Goshie had turned to me and asked, 'Where should we go next?'

'I reckon we should hit Spain!' I replied.

'Fuck that, we're not flying to South America!' he whined.

Goshie and I have been best friends since the day when, as twelve year olds, we were forced to sit next to each other on the first day of high school. At that time his little sister was just learning to talk and we would take time teaching her the names of famous skateboarders. Now we hit on girls years younger than her—times sure do change.

When choosing best friends in pre-pubescence, there are few things you think about other than how accessible their backyards are via bike, how advanced their video game collections are, how responsive they are to poorly crafted racist and gay jokes, and their ability to rip out a fart at the perfect time. One thing you do not think about is how their sleeping habits will affect your ability to enjoy the great wide world.

Goshie, you see, is a snorer. More than that, he is the worst freaking snorer imaginable. His average night's sleep sounds like when a teenage boy gets curious about what it would feel like to stick his dick in the waste disposable unit. I've slept in the same bed more than once with only three people, and he is one of them. I have slept in the same room as this guy hundreds of times, way more than anyone I have had a romantic or sexual relationship with.

So we were in Spain sharing the spare room of an old lady's house with a French man, a guy from California and two beautiful young Swedish girls, when Goshie decided to cook us all pasta for dinner. After stuffing ourselves full of Bolognese, it was time for me to hold up a deal Goshie and I had agreed upon months earlier; he who cooks relaxes for the rest of the night and tries to impress any Scandinavian girls in the hostel with his Australian accent, whereas he who does not cook but does eat is in charge of the dishes.

Only on this particular night we had been getting into the cheap Spanish wine at the same time and our heads were already buzzing, and we had been socializing, and we had plans to party that night till one of us passed out in a random back alley, so I piled the dishes high in the sink, like a dripping-red Leaning Tower of Pisa, and ran the water over the catastrophe zone until the sink was full of orange, greasy water and floating pasta bits, and I decided to take care of the dishes in the morning.

At five the next morning, I woke up and remembered something; the old lady's only rule was 'keepa thingsa cleana or kicka outa!' (And I apologize for the stereotypical borderline racist accent, also I think that's Italian not Spanish, is it still racism if you get the race wrong?) I had left a sink full of dishes, and I am not a clean freak by any nature, or even a daily clean underwear wearer, if I am being honest, but I am a loyal man, and I did not want to get any of my friends kicked out of the hostel. Well, to be slightly more honest, the two Swedish girls were both quite attractive. The day before, we had all been on the beach with them in bikinis, and one of them demonstrated just how skinny she was by nestling her bikini waistband over the top of her two protruding hip bones, leaving a good inch-deep gap between bikini material and skin, right at the beginning of her well manicured pubic hair. So it was that three of us boys spent the best part of the day surrounded by plenty of topless Spanish girls and tourists, as well as our eighteen-year-old Swedish friend giving us a literal doorway to the next logical goal when leering at women. We all got sunburned backs, but the sun never saw our fronts. When you are in board shorts and have no shirt on, there is no way to hide what you are really thinking other than burying it in the sand. We also made plans to attempt to spend some time perhaps an inch or two further down her landing strip, and in a pre-dawn, can't sleep through the snoring assault, alcohol-fueled paranoid haze, I was quite sure that getting her kicked out of her accommodation would not help me get any part of myself inside of her.

I needed to clean those goddamn dishes. I climbed out of bed, feeling awful, about to get my hands into a pool of rich tomato-flavored water. Only, I did not find a pool of water with floating dishes, as the water had drained out and the leftover pasta was now caked over all the dishes. Turns out we must have had more leftovers than I had thought; now I might get in trouble for not saving them for breakfast. When backpacking on a tight budget, throwing out perfectly good food is very much frowned upon. Every movie that has a character that is an alcoholic has one common scene, the one where the protagonist goes searching through his hoard of bottles trying to find one that still has some booze swimming at the bottom. This scene sucks, because it is not true; alcoholics don't leave half a bottle of alcohol lying around, they drink that shit, they are alcoholics! Well, backpackers and food are nothing like that, but I have always wanted to whine about those scenes and thought this was as good a time as ever.

Unfortunately, I could not find a sponge or cleaning utensil anywhere, so as I dug into the sink to pull out spaghetti and sauce-covered plates and pots, it dawned on me that I was to be cleaning these stupid things with my hands, and it was going to take some time. I began to scrub these things with my fingers, pressing hard to acquire some friction. I picked off dried-up bits of onion with my fingernails, and scooped out deeper chunks of food congregating in deep pockets. It took a long time and I was not having the slightest bit of fun, but it was my job. I got the place looking clean enough, rinsed off the last memories of dinner from my hands, wiped them dry on my dirty boxer short-covered ass, and climbed wearily back into bed.

However, before I was able to drift back to sleep, the snoring next to me ceased for a moment. Then I heard Goshie whisper across at me, 'Are you awake?'

'Sort of,' I whispered back.

'Hey, don't go near the sink, when we came home last night I had the worst spew in there!' he said with a chuckle. 'Oh my god!'

Oh, I never did get to have sex with either of the Swedish girls, although Goshie once talked them into a backyard wet t-shirt competition at a time when I wasn't around. That bastard. And he didn't even know Spain was in Europe! (I once thought a good way to build my own boxing bag was to tie a rolled up mattress onto a hanging light fitting. No one is perfect here).

Grossness is of course a relative thing. I have done and been subjected to lots and lots and lots of purely vile, disgusting, puke-inducing moments in my life, but this past couple of weeks something happened to me that has assassinated the recollection of all of them by being the grossest thing that will *ever* happen to me.

As mentioned, I have a really unhealthy diet and I like to eat huge amounts of food, which means for me, how can I say this meekly or in a nice way? Well, my body is prone to occasionally produce let's say, a lazy little hemorrhoidal growth from taking shits so big they tear the skin around asshole and then get affected as I rub shit into the wounds.

My diet recently has been particularly bad, and the toilet paper in my house has been particularly sandpapery. Put it this way, If I was gay and wanted to get fucked I'd be totally FUCKED! My ass is a fucking war zone.

Obviously this is embarrassing and not something you want to share with a bunch of strangers, so when you go to purchase the cream to remedy it, you like a good ambiguous name like Preparation H, or Sun Don't Shine Relief Cream, but where I'm from in Australia, we get the most subtle name of all—Anusol!

WHO named that?

AND NOW A FUN DAY IN A BOARDROOM, by Dave

'Hello everybody, well as you know us here at Stifle Pharmaceuticals is ready to join the exciting world of hemorrhoid relief creams'

(WARM APPLAUSE ALL AROUND)

'Yes, yes, it's a big day for those of us who have been here at Stifle for many years, and they said we'd never make it up the butt!!!!!'

(NOW RIOTOUS APPLAUSE)

'Bravo, bravo!'

'Of course for every great idea comes a problem, and here is no exception.'

'What could ever be the problem, boss sir?'

'That's a great question, teenage 1920s employee, and I'll tell you, we have no idea what to name our new product.'

'Sir, I am John Leed from accounts, I have an idea.'

'Yes John, let's hear it.'

'Well it goes on your anus, why not anus cream?'

(WARM APPLAUSE)

'Wow, that is FANTASTIC! Quick meeting, lock it in!'

'Sir, Sir, Cameron Flicks, head of marketing here, sir, please, we cannot market something named Anus Cream!'

'Wow, Cameron, you may be right, it needs to be more jazzy, and more medical, and so subtle that people can buy it without letting everyone clearly know they have a problem with their anus, wait, wait, wait, I have it—Anusol!'

(HUGE APPLAUSE)

'Cameron, what do you think?'

'Oh my god that's genius sir, I'll get working on the TV commercial right away!'

'Wait, no one is going to point out that "Anusol" is equally as embarrassing as "Anus Cream"'?

'Shut up Dave, you're fired. Good news 1920s employee, you're getting his job'

'Geewilikers sir boss, man... I'll do a bang up job, darn tooting I will'

(WARM APPLAUSE ALL AROUND)

'Got a jingle yet Cameron?'

'Yes sir, "Anusol, Anusol, Anusol, Anusol, it's a cream that goes on sores on your anus, but purchasable without embarrassment because you now have 'ol' on your anus... ANUSOL'"

(NOW RIOTOUS APPLAUSE)

That of course was merely a dramatization of what may have happened in the boardroom, the truth is these were the names they in actuality rejected:

- Ass Bleeding Balm.
- Ripped Rectum Relief.
- If Problems Persist See A Doctor In Case It's Anal Herpes Cream

AND NOW HERE IS HOW THIS PARTICULAR *FIST-SIZED* HEMORRHOIDAL GROWTH HAS BEEN AFFECTING ME by Dave

I'd been trying to drop some weight after the ridiculous amount of party-inspired indulgence over the summer that had me back to being a borderline fat guy, and this pulsating gargoyle in my pants was not going to stop me going to my building's gym. This led to two days of painful, painful gym sessions wearing multiple layers of underwear worried about this thing bursting in a show of such grossness I'd have to sell my apartment.

After this, the inevitable happened. The hemorrhoid got so big that it reached critical mass and exploded in a bloody mess the likes of which I had never seen. I began mopping out my butt with fists full of tissues trying to blot up the blood. I took showers and blood ran down my leg and saturated the floor like the stab scene from *Psycho*. There was so much blood that when nausea took over my body and made me fall to the floor, I wasn't sure if it was from my pathetic lack of ability to deal with the sight of my own blood or such heavy blood loss that I would be found dead, lying under the streaming water.

A day later I was due to fly to Canada. I had only booked days earlier, so I couldn't pull out without some major explanation, which I just did not want to give, so I took my bags, luggage variety and bloody variety, and headed to the airport. This thing was now bleeding consistently, needing attention at least every couple of hours, so I needed to take my Anusol on the plane, meaning I got to go through security worrying about this:

'Hey, hippie hair, come over here, we need to check your bag for drugs. What's this, Anusol? You been smoking pot, getting the munchies so bad that the turds you do rip your asshole, or have you just been getting fucked in the ass by lots of dudes?'

'Um um, I feel like I should say the second one?'

'Well, you're lucky you jerk, because I should cavity search you, but I ain't going anywhere near whatever is wrong with your ass.'

Perfectly Positive Bear: Good news for people with regular hemorrhoid problems—if you ever try and make anal love to a girl and she says 'what if it bleeds after?' You can say, 'Don't worry, baby, I don't go anywhere without Anusol!'

On the plane, for some God-only-knows reason, while already grossed out beyond belief by my own ass, I decided to watch the incredible film *127 Hours,* about the true story of Aaron Ralston, who cut off his own arm after getting it trapped under a boulder. Oh my God. As it ended, I was shaking with joy and fear and trying my hardest not to cry myself into a blathering mess. I actually had to get up, line up for the bathroom, and then let myself explode into a snotty mess all alone. It really inspired me to remember my lust for life, unencumbered by my neurotic bullshit. Wow—life, man. Hell yeah!

Then again, I couldn't help but think these things:

1. Once this guy's food and drink ran out, why didn't he masturbate and drink his own jizz?
2. This movie comes with a warning: 'Contains scenes that SOME flyers may find disturbing.' It shows a man

graphically chopping off his own arm, if there are ANY people on my plane who do NOT find that disturbing, I guarantee they have eaten, for pleasure, at least one other human being.

3. Even though I knew in advance how it ended, once he had chopped off his arm and escaped, I kind of really wanted to see him fall again and trap his other arm, that's how disturbed my mind is.

4. While I was in the bathroom crying over this man's heroic act of courage, I also performed my own act of bloody courageous self-medical care as I replaced one hemorrhoid bloody tissue sheet from my ass crack and jammed up my ass a fresh one. Maybe we really do all have heroes inside us!

This was the flight taking me to the previously mentioned Whistler skiing trip. I love skiing, but I really wasn't sure if I could handle it. No matter how much Preparation H and/or Anusol I threw up there, it bled like a gunshot wound for day after day after day. Plus, it really, really hurt, especially with legs-being-pulled-apart skiing falls. It was a throbbing yet also stabbing pain.

As it was, I did ski, only in a way that required bathroom breaks to change out the bloody tissues soaking in my ass at least every hour or two. I had come here to go heli-skiing, where they throw you out of a helicopter so you can ski the steep, hard ungroomed mountains of the backcountry, but instead I'd have volunteered to clean up vomit in every rehab center on earth to be gifted one day of relief from this dreadfulness, but alas, it was, once again just my destiny to face the unlucky consequences of my disregard for my body. For the record, friends who were there that may have been offended that I was the only one who did not take off underpants for our streaking, trust me: you didn't want to see what I was hiding under there.

Next was on to Portland, where I risked further wrath, with my donut feast having to come out again eventually, but in my defense, while I already complained about Valentine's Day in Portland, what I didn't mention is that as I walked around I began to hope I would get mugged, so in my anger I could pretend to go for my wallet but instead whip out a fist full of bloody tissues from my ass then scream, 'YOU want what I've got? Well I have AIDS so bad my ass bleeds! You want this, motherfucker? you want this motherfucker?'

For the record, I am writing this chapter while in hiding from a hotel lobby after overflowing my hotel room toilet and requesting an emergency room servicing because of a need for 'towels'. I really, really doubt I will ever be a proper adult. I mentioned before that my being in the mountains re-inspired my need for adventure, and it did, but why did it have to be marred with such disgusting horror? Has this duality of good and bad I have been chasing with all these memory killings forced my mind to *always* create good with bad or bad with good?

If you choose to, you may remember that this issue continued to haunt me for what transpired in at least the next three chapters, or instead you may choose to remember that at least I'm not the kind of guy just to leave dirty dishes that were my responsibility for someone else to find, so that's a good thing about me, right?

SOMETIMES IT JUST IS FATE

Here are some more examples of the kind of thoughts I sometimes let run through my brain, and unfortunately sometimes can't help but verbalize or write on social media sites, even knowing as I do it that I'll hate myself for it in the morning.

'I've been desperately keen on the ol' opposite sex for twenty-plus years and in that time I have been helplessly attracted to 100 girls a day, yet never felt that in my direction once. 100 x 365 x 20 = 730,000. That's how many people I have felt rejected by!'

'Yet to really sum up my ridiculous problem is this. I love/crave/need/dream of unique creative people, and I choose to look different in hope of avoiding the boring people and finding the cool people. It means for the most part I voluntarily avoid my own attractiveness and yet I get pissed off all the bloody time that people don't find me attractive. And I mean the very same people I don't actually want to meet. It's a self-fulfilling prophecy of the most stupid manner'

'99% of chicks are whores and yet I still don't have whatever they want'

The weird thing is I know I will hate myself in the morning for posting that crap this BUT I am still having fun in the moment. It's like a little rant to make sure I know that tomorrow will suck so 'enjoy now, you idiot'.

Wait, wait, back up a little. Since I last wrote about it, I totally relapsed on anti-depression medication. I was feeling awful and so went pill chasing and got left numb again.

So I again had to attempt to wean myself off. A couple of months off max dose and hello, psycho up and down Dave was back. I found myself gleaming with the inspiration that comes from being alone, travelling, just letting my surroundings take over the imagination part of my brain, unaffected by censors or filters I throw up while facilitating the 'expectations' I impose upon myself around people who already know me.

The sexuality that is revived in me once medication-free had me promising myself to have the 'balls' to 'get out of my system' a few sexual fantasies by screwing hookers in Vegas and telling you all about it in the hope it'll allow me to shamefully accept the possibility of actually letting a girl into my heart without all the doubt and 'what will this mean I'll never get to do' stupidity racing through my mind.

But then I started dreaming of having a partner, by which I mean an actual partner, not just a user of my generosity. Today I am feeling desperate to merely hold a girl's hand and for that to mean *everything* to her. By the time I was sane enough to have girls genuinely be part of my life, they had all outgrown this immensely sweet and adorable phase. Boyfriends became just another in a string, and I never liked being 'just another' of anything in life. I want something special.

Tomorrow I'll probably return to craving, or at least imagining, wickedly wild sex, group sex, groupie sex, and crazy treat-my-body-like-a-playground sex.

Living between these two vastly contradictory fantasies and never getting anywhere with either, combined with the fact that the few break ups I've had have been mortifying, soul crushing, heart shatteringly bad (mostly because of my own pathetically morbid inability to cope with rejection), leaves me feeling utterly alone, bitter and yet constantly convinced I am rejected by EVERY woman I encounter. A girl with a boyfriend silently screams at me 'you weren't worth waiting for'. She chose him over me even though we had never met. Why am I so worthless? I find myself attracted to hundreds of girls a day and attempt eye contact and smiles with them all. The fact that 99.999999% of them don't reciprocate makes me feel like a weed, with no thought to what she is doing, thinking or feeling, or to the fact she is just another random in my whoring of instant crushes. Also, the fact that if she doesn't match up to either of my ridiculous ideals listed above, ultimately it'll be me who rejects her, and if she does I'll hate her for not being the other. As you can see, my dreams are a vicious, totally unsatisfactory cycle of oxymoron piled onto oxymoron that I can't fathom how to break. How do you get what you want when it changes drastically day after day, moment after moment?

I wrote this originally on the plane, having met up with a friend on our way to Los Angeles. I knew we were going to party down there, and party hard. Yet I was secretly writing this and thinking, 'I don't know how to tell you, buddy. We've had some awesome simply decadent times together. When we party we have a way of inspiring each other into breaking all the natural rules of what kind of crazy fun and mischief we can get up to. But mate, I think I'm over it, I know it will disappoint you, but this time in LA I'm going to take it a little easy, I'm dreaming of something different at the moment, I want to find an innocent sweetheart to love.' The following is the true story of what happened AFTER I wrote and thought the above.

We arrived to our motel on Sunset in Hollywood, and while tired, my mate and I are reminiscing about one year ago today, when as people who barely knew each other we coincidentally came together in this wonderful town and proceeded to tear it a new asshole. As we were given our room key, we had two things on our minds—get showered, then get out on the town.

As we literally kicked open the door to our room, let's say a problem was in there; it was a literally a porn star, dressed all porned-up sexy, while another porn star lay on the bed and a guy in the background set up lighting rigs.

'Um, hello.'

'Who are you guys?'

'I think we were given the wrong room.'

We all had a laugh, and I was mesmerized by this model's tattooed-covered half-exposed gorgeous body and after a brief conversation they invited us to a party later, with the promise of 'no cover just lots of porn stars' and I thought, 'There is no way I can be happy with one girl in my life with that out there unexplored!'

We got to our real room, laughing all the way at the dumb cold unlikeliness of what had just happened. I've stayed in a lot of motels, hotels and hostels, and this is the ONLY time I have been given the wrong key, so finding a porn set just about to be attacked was absolutely nuts!

Here is how the rest of the night unfolded:

- We leave the motel and look up at her room window, only to see hundreds of flashes from cameras going off! Why didn't we walk in 5 minutes later?
- We have some drinks and then nice and boozed up we head to the party where, sure enough, she is there, and so are a whole slew of porn-industry types.
- I ask the original porn star about what her chest/boob tattoo is all about and she tells me it means 'fucking in the mouth, pussy and ass is all good to me'.
- My friend asks her if she can still get excited about having sex with a new love interest and she says she gets more excited about snuggles and asks him if she can film the two of them snuggling for a project she is doing, something he turns DOWN. So she kisses him on the mouth.
- I get insanely jealous, in both interpretations of that sentence, then people keep buying me drinks and I get insanely drunk.
- We go back the motel, where they have moved the after party two rooms away from ours, so we turn up

and it's overflowing with drugs, sex and wall-to-wall guys lusting over two porn stars.

- I have a brief attempt to crack onto one of the porn stars and get nowhere so head to bed dejected.
- My friend gets 'in' with the other one, and thinks 'if I just asked her to fuck me in the bathroom, she'd probably just do it, I mean what's it to her, then again some of these big beefy druglord types might not like it and beat me up'. He then spends days regretting not at least asking.
- The next morning we walk past their room hoping to see them again but cleaners are in the room, they have checked out.
- So I jump on the Internet and within moments have found her, and watch numerous videos of people treating her body just in the same way my deepest fantasies have been doing a few hours earlier. Her name is Coco Velvett, and she is a genuine star.
- We head to the IHOP across the road for breakfast and over the course of five minutes I discover my friend had gotten her number, and I can totally use my book as an excuse to try and have some sort of 'experience' with her. So I text her over my plate of pancakes, asking if I can be filmed snuggling on camera with her for her project or if she can suggest some sort of other 'crazy experience'.
- I hit send, look up, and see a mop of blonde hair. Holy crap, she is sitting in the very same restaurant as we speak.
- My friend says, 'Go talk to her, man.' I say, 'I can't go up to a porn star in IHOP and say remember me?' He says, 'Where are your balls, man?' And I think, 'Balls? Like the ones I just watched jumping up and down while I watched videos of men having sex with her?'

- I hesitate for a long while, at one point claiming I'll do it when I have finished my food, knowing that she'll probably leave before I do.
- My friend continues to challenge me, so I do it. I nervously get up and go over there, and say, 'Hi, remember me?'
- Within seconds her manager, who is sitting with her, pulls out his phone and says, 'Yeah man, last night was great, wasn't it? Check out the photos. ' Then he shows me hundreds of photos of the naked vagina of the girl sitting right there, as well as lots of other nude shots of her and other porn stars, many taken in the club last night while we were there. How did we miss that?
- We have a brief chat, but Coco is clearly as hung over as all hell, so I give a little pitch for this book, tell them if they have any ideas of things for me to do let me know, and I go back to eat.
- I see them get up and leave in the distance, but then the manager comes running back in from outside just to tell us that there is a porn set getting set up as we speak, and, like Batman, Coco has been summoned for immediate porn work, so they must rush off. He smiles the smile of a man who knows that what he does may not be respected or high profile, but he has left two Aussie boys sitting at a table at IHOP dripping with envy for how he lives his life.
- I think, 'My God, what I would give to bang her,' and then, 'Still, I really do just want to hold a special girl's hand.'

I'm trying to have a normal relationship with women, I really am, yet what does it mean when just as I am thinking these things fate thrusts me into a world of porn? Also, sorry 99% of chicks, I don't really think you are whores, I just want you to love me.

IN THE PAST FEW YEARS I'VE BOASTED I'M INCAPABLE OF BEING BORED

The retardation of my existence is boundless.

The boys and I headed out for a night on the famed Sunset Strip. I LOVE this area. As a student of the rock and the rolls, this place is like what casinos are to people who like to make large donations to people who already have lots of money. It's two blocks where like ninety percent of the greatest moments in music history have taken place. We of course were there hoping to meet girls.

So we were at the Rainbow Bar and Grill having a lovely dinner, pumping each other up for a night of drinking and debauchery, when a woman came and cuddled right up to me in my booth and with sign language, touch and innuendo said to me, 'Please take me to the nearest bed and treat my body like a beer fridge!' (I probably don't need to translate this, but I want to - Open me up and stick lots of fat, spherical-type dealies in me, ok? Sorry). I've been fantasizing about a moment like this for so long and I, and the boys, were all so dumb-founded when it actually happened, that this women actually responded out loud, 'Are you all deaf-mute?' to which we thought she must have thought we were in a band called 'Deaf-Mute' that must be so huge that women throw themselves at.

Yet it wasn't that, she just wanted to bang me—AND I TURNED HER DOWN!

In my defense, she was WAY older than me, and I'm rarely attracted to anyone even the same age as me, and she was riddled with plastic surgery, and if I am going to have a handful of rubber I want to be changing a flat tire on a spooky road at 4am in a snow storm, not having some lady saying to me, 'You like my breasts?'

Sorry, lady, you don't HAVE breasts anymore. (PS – fake-boobed ladies, please feel free to try to convince me otherwise, and hey, be creative!)

Still, I don't have any business turning these kinds of offers down. I'm a starving kid in Cambodia; I can't say this cut of meat is not my favorite.

So we saw a couple of bands at the Roxy, where there was a cute little artsy rocker chick who I thought may be looking at me until she ended up blowing a female load over the bassist in a super crap band.

We moved on to the Cat Club, where for the second time of the night we were able to NOT pay the cover charge because we promised to drink a lot, a bouncer practice that had us salivating and jumping with joy and laughing about how awesome the nightlife is in LA, until the next place, Happy Endings, a college pick-up bar, where we didn't get let in because we were too drunk. What the hell?

So we had to prove this wrong. 'No way are we too drunk, let's prove to ourselves just how much more alcohol we are capable of consuming!' It was now only an hour from bar closing time, we didn't know any others close by, but we could see the bright lights of a strip club only a block away. We went and drank like maniacs. Also, the girls in this strip club didn't strip, they just stripped down to bikinis. On the other hand, one particular stripper covered head to toe in tattoos seemed to take a liking to me, and after her performance she sat down next to me and proceeded to have a really cool conversation. When we left at closing, she actually ran over to me and gave me a big hug. I was smitten. Why does my brain do these things?

By now we really were boozed up hard. Our retaliation mission against Happy Endings meant we had about six shots each and a couple of cocktails, and upon leaving we had a bizarre incident of running into a man who called himself 'Big LA' who was eating a pack of Lays chips, allowing the boys and I to keep saying over and over, 'Lazy Lays, lazy sweet onion and cheese, lazy night lazing around eating Lays,' then we went to another strip club where girls did strip and the booze didn't exist.

By now we were drunk enough to be taken advantage of. My credit card and driver's license were taken hostage, and I was taken to a back room where girls were thrust upon me, and this is the honest truth, I didn't enjoy one second of it. At one point one of the girls angrily turned to me and said, 'I can't believe two girls are fucking on you and you look that bored.'

I just wanted it to end, and when it finally did the bill was astronomical, almost like tweeting with international data roaming on expensive! (I just accidently wrote 'expenis') I complained and was told, 'We have your credit card and driver's license and if you don't sign your bill I can make life very hard for you.' When I suggested I'd have been happier to pay if the show was any good, I was told, 'Tell you what, I'll get you another girl and then I'll take those two out the back and fuck them up.' He then continued to kindly offer to 'punch the girls in the face' several times, but I just signed the fucking bill and ran for my life.

After getting out of this hellhole, I knew I couldn't sleep, so despite it being four in the morning I went for a walk, just wondering what the hell is wrong with my life.

As I often do, I pulled out my phone to write notes to myself to remember this moment, and how this sort of debauched rock n' roll lifestyle is an awesome fantasy but the reality is that it's cold, and gross, and somehow actually boring.

I wrote to myself to remember that if I allowed love to be an option to me I'd be happier, more sane and save thousands and thousands of dollars.

Having typed this into my phone I felt better for a moment, like I had turned a corner, and with that done I wanted to get my mind off it, and stop bashing myself for what an idiot I had been. I fell into a weird pit of laughter for a moment, thinking about where I was, in Hollywood, having just experienced my Motley Crue moment. I'd lived out one of the songs I had sung along with a million times as a shy teenager dreaming of having the confidence and lifestyle of these rock gods. And I hated it. The truth was hilarious.

It was at this moment I decided to check my emails, and there it was—an email from my ex; a happy little email with her abusing me because apparently I had spent so much money on her that the IRS was chasing her for tax evasion. Love saves me money?

The retardation of my existence is boundless.

A week later I was once again invited to the porn party and late that night I stood in a small yet packed motel room in Hollywood and watched as porn star Coco Velvett received oral sex from another woman, and did it bore me? Hell no, instead it got me so turned on that on the way home I drunk dialed a platonic friend in a desperate, and for some unknown reason, unsuccessful attempt at some sort of booty call.

The retardation of my existence is, well you get the point.

Also, having just changed in the bathroom for the first time in days away from the harsh light of the motel room, I discovered that I did have a huge bloodstain on the seat of my pants from my little issue from a couple of chapters back. It had been a like a week since it last really bled hard, so I'd been walking around like that all week!

When I found it, I didn't suddenly think back to the myriad of people who perhaps saw it and didn't say anything because what do you say when you see someone has an ass bloodstain? I didn't for a second think about all the conversations people may have had speculating on what exactly I had been up to. I am not even thinking about those things as I am writing this. No, all I did was see blood in my jeans, flip them over to confirm it had soaked through, then chuckled to myself and thought 'that is actually kind of funny'. My existence is retarded, but I think I might actually be maturing!

MY MIND IS A BABBLING TODDLER

Clearly, my mind is retarded. And I don't mean in a un-PC joking kind of way, I mean in a 'mental retardation is a generalized disorder appearing before adulthood, characterized by significantly impaired cognitive functioning and deficits in two or more adaptive behaviors' – Wikipedia, kind of way.

Adaptive behaviors, in my case, are that my mind just won't shut up. Not even for a moment. For the most part, this is a good thing. As a writer it means I am inundated with ideas to draw upon, and often times this has even meant I have climbed into bed, thinking I would have a night's sleep like a normal person, and instead found myself at the computer at 4am, a place I would stay until a third of a novel was written. Two or three weeks later, a complete novel would have poured out of me that is so brilliant and original and thought provoking that to this day not one agent nor publisher will dare read a single word, knowing that should these books be published the entire world of entertainment will be changed forever, and believing that even if they are the ones to discover me, this kind of revolution is too much for the world to handle right now. Those publishing types really are generous to the world.

As I am supposed to be changing my negative attitudes, I have decided to mentally decide I am brilliant. Why the hell not? Ah, so positive. I do actually believe I am brilliant, at a minimum of twelve times every day. At least twelve times a day I also think I suck, am average, am just coming into my own, would do better if I did 'A, B or C', to wow that girl has a nice ass, to I need to change career to 'D, E, F, G, or H' because that's where my real talent lies, I wish I was born a kitten, hey I might go get some pizza anyone want any? Yeah right, like I'm not going to eat the whole thing myself. Also, when I am not thinking these things, my mind actually changes its opinions, topics, thoughts, likes, dislikes and current feelings again, and again, and again.

It's the source of my insomnia, why I became a writer, why sometimes people think I am not listening to them, and why I have checked emails and read an article online while writing this story, all while sitting in a diner people-watching everyone in the room and wondering what to have for dinner even though I have only just put down my fork after finishing lunch.

One thing I have never done, and have just been inspired to attempt, is for one day to try and note down literally every thought I have. Let's try it, starting now:

- I just thought don't think about bad stuff, then
- I imagined a train hitting a car, then
- Why do I always imagine violent stuff, then
- Oh crap, the guy next to me who has been a whiney asshole since he came in, just confessed to the girl he is with that he decided to date a girl he's known for ages, even though she has two kids, and he hates kids so much he has actively encouraged two of his exes to have abortions, then
- Shit, too many responses to his confession flying at me like a flock of migrating geese, to even get close to getting them down
- Don't do it
- Either of you
- Why would anyone say stuff like this in a restaurant
- Wow, now he says they are having an open relationship
- I don't think I have ever heard a Flock of Seagulls song

- My God, I wasn't even supposed to be starting writing every thought down, this was just supposed to be a preliminary test
- Oh my God, now he says and this girl is pregnant with his kid and they are going to keep it
- No, seriously, is he doing that
- Train hitting car
- Train hitting car
- Stop thinking violent stuff, stop it stop it
- Train hitting car
- He's fondling his friend's arm, sexually. I have a really horrible feeling that even though I am only semi-listening he is confessing all this to his friend because he is actually telling her he wants to date her too, and she seems to be responding in the positive
- Four million thoughts of girls I wish I could have been with and he is actually telling a girl he is seeing someone else, she is pregnant, but they are in an open relationship and he wants to see her too, and it's working
- Too many bloody thoughts to possibly write down
- Don't think about violent stuff
- Don't think about violent stuff
- Flashing images of babies being punched, war, car crashes, miscellaneous violence in my head, babies being stepped on in the face
- That guy Jesse James cheated on and humiliated his wife Sandra Bullock and within months he's upgraded (in my mind) to Kat Von D. What's wrong with the world, surely being outed to the world as alleged Nazi sympathizing adulterous scum guarantees a lifetime of loneliness, or at least a relocation to a third-world Asian country to find a partner
- Sixty times a day I see a girl and think, 'Why can't I get a girl like that?' so how could I ever even contemplate finding the 'one'?
- I should buy cashews before I go home

- Fuck there is no Diet Dr Pepper in Australia, I don't want to live there
- Now you're just thinking things you often think because you're thinking about thinking and therefore thinking about things you think
- Seriously dude, you've talked two girls into getting abortions, and now you're using the information that you have impregnated a mother of two to hit on a girl literally three minutes after complaining about how long your sandwich was taking to cook
- Goddamn it, thought overload, I can't keep this up
- Abort, Abort, Abort
- Not as in an abortion, as in abort this stupid idea
- Ok

Seriously, that was less than a minute of thoughts, and only a fraction of the thoughts I had in that time. Holy shit.

In this time I also kept thinking the words 'tennis', 'helmet', 'rape' and 'AIDS' over and over. Those four words, for no reason I can deduce, are on the top of my mind these days, all day, every day. If my mind is literally like a babbling toddler, then I don't know WHAT these kids are going to grow up to become!

Maybe I need to stop thinking about all the things I'm always thinking about, or come to think about it, just stop thinking. I think I should learn to meditate, but I don't think I would be capable of it, now my mind is just thinking over and over again, 'Stop thinking about thinking, stop thinking about thinking.' I need to walk away from this computer NOW!

With my adventurous spirit re-awakened, I decided to something I had long dreamed of and get the train all the way across the United States. I have crossed the continent six or seven times by car, at least as many times by plane, and I have gone halfway by train, but with rail travel my absolute favorite form of travel, it was time to go the whole hog. Also, I get a weird pleasure from depriving myself of things. No bed, privacy, decent food options, parties, TV, or Internet for a few days—count me in.

As is evident in the past few pages, my neurotic blathering mind had been getting way out of control recently. I decided this train ride might be a good time to try something different. My rule for this train ride was that every time I began to try and think of the big picture things I want or don't want, things I like or don't like, things about Dave, David, David Tieck and the other twenty-four unnamed personalities in my head, I had to stop, breath, remember where I was, enjoy what was outside the window, and be in the moment. This was going to be tough.

I arrived at the train station about four hours early. Why? I still have no idea. What I do know is that the staff at Amtrak at Union Station in Los Angeles are so rude and incompetent that I no longer feel bad for unemployed people; if you can't convince someone you'd be better at a job than *these* people, then you really do have some problems.

I eventually climbed onto the train, with night already having fallen. I was sat next to a 'big fat red back', as he called himself; an NRA-card-carrying, highly vocal Republican, who wanted to tell me all his political ideals before the train got out of Los Angeles. Actually, he turned out to be really nice, funny, insightful and very respectful of the political views that were different than his. Then he bought me beer. Yay. Still, I didn't want to talk politics and be squashed for forty-eight hours.

I tried to go to the snack car to reciprocate the beer buying, and as I arrived a bunch of drunks got into a fistfight right in front of me. Being the hero that I am, I right away helped get a couple of girls out of the way and up the stairs then stood back trying to block them from harm, before the blond German woman that worked at the snack bar jumped on top of them to try and break the fight up, and everyone looked at me like, 'You left it for a woman to do that? What kind of a man are you?' *Oh shit, it's less than three hours into the trip, I am on a train that's already breaking into violence. I'm never going to sleep and everyone thinks I am a wimp or a misogynist or both.*

'Live in the moment, Dave.'

'Ok, AAUUUAGGHHHHHHHHHH!!!!! What have I got myself into?'

Then a miracle. A super, super nice and friendly Amtrak staff member defied all odds and found me a double seat to myself (sometimes it's good when drunks fight, because the train stops to have them arrested and their seats come up for grabs).

With a couple of beers in my belly, and a big comfy seat to myself, I curled up into a ball and thought, 'Look where you are, on a crazy adventure, around interesting people and things. Stop freaking trying to manipulate things, just be in the moment,' and I fell into a train-rockingly beautiful sleep.

I woke up to a bright orange sunrise over the glorious red rock and snow-peppered Arizonan Desert, while an Amish man next to me videotaped it with the latest phone technology from Apple. He had a GPS machine on the table and was wearing crocs, three of the most enthusiastically loved products that people can't help but complain about but heavily adopt in the 21st century. You go, Amish. That's living in the moment hard core.

From here on in, everything was magnificent. I saw the desert and snow, small towns and countryside, rivers and mountains, and I really was feeling in the moment. This was wonderful; every time I caught myself, it made me smile warmly, 'Stop, breathe, remember now, how awesome is this! Hey, you're smiling again!'

I saw a huge magnificent bald eagle as we crossed the Mississippi into Illinois, the state of Lincoln; three of the greatest symbols of a great nation coming together. I read two books. I listened to awesome music. I got really inspired to write. I was going to say all the ways I failed miserably in my 'don't think about the past or future' goal, but screw that; this was just good. That's all that needs to be said.

I had begun to think that my hopes from this mind expedition of mine were deteriorating miserably. Like I said earlier, I felt like not dealing with my past was holding me back from a successful future, but dealing with it hadn't seemed to be working either. Yet suddenly I was feeling some clarity. From babbling non-sensically,

I am back to bubbling with enthusiasm. I just need to say it—yay, yay, yay, yay, yay, yay!

Also, I learned a lot on this train trip, such as:

- Note to parents: when your kid is on the floor bawling its NOT trying to say -ignore me ignore me I don't want parental love ignore me PLEASE.
- Dave Tieck's mind is equal to a forty-nine inch penis, just be glad you have neither deep inside of you.
- A Victoria secret model is equal to murder; it's not worth the fantasy.
- The whites of the eye are equal to saying 'hello governor', both would be massively desirable if coming out of a Victoria secret models vagina.
- A slam dunk is equal a to bowl of chili, you make either in a fish tank & PETA hates you.
- The missionary position is equal to a shot of tequila. Give either to a 9yo and there is something wrong with your morals. Plus I'm here ladies!
- Making love to a Victoria's secret model is equal to a bear licking your ear lobe. If no one else saw it, then it didn't happen.
- A happy birthday sign is equal to a glass of water. Pull either out of your underpants and you wear way too big underpants.
- Snow is equal to a plasma TV, stick enough of either up your nose and you'll wish you were born in Argentina.
- Food packaging has nutritional facts but never fun facts: phili-cream cheese one serve is known to spray at various angles & destroy your book.
- 'I've never paid child support; I'm always in jail' from a mom of 3 and 'I'm off work at the moment because I punched my friend and broke my arm in three places'

equal the two most disturbing things overheard on the train.

- Forty three hours on train, now in Chicago with heavy snow falling, not sure what's a more pressing thought - lack of coat, need for shower, desire for deep-dish pizza, or desire to possess a forty-nine inch penis?

WELL BLOW ME
DOWN, SHIRLEY

So, I was hanging out in a remote park near a friend of mine's house late at night one weekend. We were seventeen and my friend was planning on sneaking out so we could get up to no good (we were going to go buy hotdogs at a gas station, we were hardcore), but abruptly my plans changed.

Of all places, at this park in the middle of nowhere, that few people knew about, the girl I had the biggest crush on in my life suddenly drove up and parked right near me. Clearly this was fate. It was destiny. Coincidence was nowhere near *this* powerful.

I looked across at her car and tried to plan my move. At this stage I had never had a conversation with a girl, but I had nervously said hello and grunted the odd thing at her, and at this time that made her the most significant relationship I had had with a girl, and in this moment the shyness sort of strangely melted away. I knew I would make my move, and it would work too, I knew it.

Then things sort of changed a little. She climbed out of her car, as did a boy in the passenger seat, and they climbed into the backseat. Hmmm. I let myself imagine a hundred things that they could have been doing other than naughty stuff; it was my imagination at its finest. But even eventually I had to give in and admit the love of my life was making love in my vicinity but I was not the owner of the penis in question, and in fact I didn't even own a penis capable of doing this to her.

So I did all I could; I sabotaged. I think I honked my horn or something, and she hastily jumped out of the back seat, jumped into the driver's seat, and crashed her (parents') Mercedes into a wooden pole. Suck it, bitch.

Now, you'd think drawing attention to myself, as someone who had just seen her fornicating and then ruined it for her, would make her fall in love with me. So later on that night, when I somehow amazingly ran into her again (man fate, you really are a horrible dude aren't you?), just in case she didn't know it was me who had been in that car ruining her night, I actually told her it was me! For some reason after that she always seemed really wary of me. Love makes girls do weird things.

Later on at a party, while she was drunk and I still didn't believe kids drank, she gave me my first real hug, and the feel of her breasts on my chest would keep me company in bed at night many times. I even made fake breasts out of foam that I put inside the pillowcase of my favorite cuddle pillow to feel something similar again. Love makes guys really normal.

Often in my life I've liked to argue that all my problems are the universe, or fate, conspiring to make me miserable. But I can't blame mother universe for my embarrassing life. The whole point of this journey was to take ownership of these stories by choosing to laugh at them and change my attitude towards them. Still, the real lesson is I could have just done that from the get go and enjoyed life. So, I was walking around Chicago, it was freezing cold, with snow on the ground, and ponds in the park frozen over. I had walked for five or six hours, been to a randomly found zoo and seen lions and tigers and bears, walked through gorgeous Lincoln Park, with views of the magnificent Chicago skyline, walked around Old Town and the Lakeview neighborhood, and saw the famed 'The Second City', the birthplace of many of mine and I'm sure your favorite comedians of all time, when I few things hit me:

1. I've been wearing a not nearly warm enough hoodie, seen at least three thousand shops today and not one sold warm winter coats, leaving me screwed, yet every other Chicagoan I've seen has been wearing a very warm-looking coat. That means if you live in Chicago warm coats must eventually magically appear on you! That's awesome.
2. I don't care if I'm cold; right now I'm deliriously happy, more so than I've been in a long time.
3. My desire to work on my artistic goals is as strong as it's ever been, so much so that I'm really contemplating flying home ASAP to just work.
4. My adventurous spirit is as strong as it's ever been, so much so that I keep fantasizing about getting on trains for days and seeing everything I can.
5. My creativity feels as wild as it did after I first took a crowbar to my brain and opened up my soul, finally letting out the ghosts and angels that had been brewing away fighting dream battles for decades. I haven't felt that for a couple of years. It's good; no, it's brilliant!
6. I'm off anti-depressants, and haven't drunk or wallowed in misery to unhealthy obsessive levels in a few weeks now, and I have no desire to do any of the above. Even if my penis still is a firecracker, if I get sex again it will be highly embarrassing, but I'll get to have sex again!
7. I'm getting healthy sleep; two weeks ago I got up one day at 7pm but since then I've been making a commitment to early starts and making the most of my days and I'm sticking to it and loving it.
8. Over the past few years I've let some toxic people into my life, recognized the signs early, but waited till they had hurt me immensely before letting go. Frankly, I've also burnt some bridges with some good friends with my own selfish, too easily hurt crazy ways, but I feel like I'm in a place where future friendships and relationships will be way healthier (until they read this book and go, 'Whoa, Nelly, I'm not hanging with this psycho.' Then again, do I want people in my life that use the phrase 'Whoa, Nelly'?)

9. Tomorrow I start a class at IO, The Second City's sister school and theater of creating and molding the best comic minds on earth, where I get to meet some cool new people and we spend a few days making each other laugh.

10. I'm feeling like I don't need to keep murdering memories much longer, and trust me I've only scraped the surface so far. Arguably the biggest are still to come, but I don't think I need it. I'm fizzy with happiness right now, and as I write this, a huge meat-covered delicious Chicago pizza was just placed in front of me in a cool pizza joint in a hidden basement of an old building in one of the coolest buildings in the world.

11. Not one girl I have had a crush on in years has had sex in the backseat of a car in front of me!

Let me say it again—yay, yay, yay, yay, yay, yay, yay!

PLEASE REPEAT YOURSELF

Growing up and well into adulthood, I've had zero faith in the words coming out of my mouth, and as such for much of my life all I dreamed about was silence.

Little known fact about silence: It was invented by Satan. Why do you think they have all those harps in heaven? It's not that anyone likes harp music, it's that they know silence means hell!

My very first fantasies about becoming an author were all about a job I could do at home, alone, with no need to talk to anyone! (Hugely false, it turns out—thank God). If I never had to talk to anyone, I never had to say a word. Wow, a job made for me. Actually, the full dream included:

- To be a writer and not have to talk.
- There would be a pill for all nutrition so you'd rarely have to eat and when you did it would only be pizza and dessert.
- Everyone would have to wear the same outfit and have the same haircut.
- There would be a machine to get me into an isolation pod at any sporting ground in the world.
- Of course, real human-looking sex robots, and
- All romantic relationships are banned (even in my have-anything fantasy world I couldn't imagine one, and if I can't have one, no one can)

I can't say I want much of that anymore. Oh, I guess I'd still like relationships banned—take the very idea of it out of our heads and we'd all be much happier. Think of all the time you'd have to read my books! I still love to write, and I am proud that I dreamed of it, even in a fantasy world where I could just as easily have dreamed of never having to work, and I'm proud I never got into it for money or fame or even critical acclaim (and yet I do have all those things, in my current fantasy world). I just knew I'd love to spend my days that way, and I do. Yet, I do still wish I actually *liked* to talk.

I remember being by my grandfather's side on his deathbed. He was a brilliant man, who at age thirteen financially supported his family during the depression, and then went on to build a fortune in the grocery game via taking on and beating the big chains by, among other things, making sure food was more affordable for everybody, and starting trends we all still benefit from today. Oh and he was a man whom I'd let shyness scare me from getting to know properly. When he was told his life was about to end, and he demanded to die at home even though it literally meant it'd be hours at best, well we feared the worst to put it lightly, and even I knew I had to be there. When I arrived at his house, I was immediately ushered into his bedroom. His nurse explained quickly and distinctly that he could go any second and I, well we, a brother, sister-in-law, and one other person who's been blocked from my memory were there, and one by one we said what we knew would be our 'final' words. I went last and froze. I was beyond self-conscious. I wanted this moment to end as fast as death could come (mine, not his). I crawled through some disgraceful small talk, looked at my companions for impossible guidance, and felt like the world's biggest fool, of all time. Why? 'Cause I was worried that the nurse, who I'd still never formally met, would think, 'Wow, I've watched a lot of people die, but never seen a loser talk to a dying person like this before!' Did I care about my Pa, the man I ultimately owe everything to? Of course I did—but love, fear, sadness, respect, decent human emotions combined, quadrupled and deep-fried compared little to my own intense natural shyness. It was pathetic. I could have just said, 'Thank you and I love you,' but I actually said something like, 'Um, so, um, yeah, how are y... um, good to see you, and um, yeah, um.' Selfish and pitiable David. Cut to ten years earlier, and it was my last day of year ten at high school and one of the last classes before our long summer hide-in-my-closet-every-day-hell-yeah break. Because no one ever pays attention on the last day of school, they tried to make it a little bit more fun, so my English teacher decided we would play theatre sports, which if you don't know are short games where people attempt to improvise scenes for comical effect.

I don't know what happened, but some combination of happiness to not have to see these asshole classmates for months and getting away from this particular teacher, who was so disgustingly bad that he made me despise books and writing for years, abruptly snapped shy Dave out of his shell and I found myself *volunteering* to participate. It was like for an hour the monkey on my back had accidently injected cocaine instead of evil sauce. And it was fun, I felt alive in way I hadn't in ages, I was even kind of good at the games. I specifically remember taking control of scenes because my loser classmates didn't have the imagination to come up with anything.

I volunteered for game after game. Even a couple of times games I distinctly disliked. A new me had just been born and I wanted to play with him. The teacher announced that for the final game of the day we would play a game called twenty questions, and my hand went up to be the center of attention and I was selected. The way this game worked was that I would stand at the blackboard, another student would come behind me and write the name of someone everyone in class should know, and then I had twenty yes or no questions to guess who the person was.

'Am I movie star?' A few snickers from the class, but no.

'Am I an athlete?' Huge laughter from the class! Ok, definitely not an athlete then, hmmm.

'Am I an actor?' Ha ha ha.

'Am I female?' More laughter. 'Practically, but no,' someone said. Ok, what the hell does that mean?

I don't remember the rest of the questions, but everything I offered was shot down with 'no's and laughter. This was a celebrity right, so was I talented at something? No, and hilariously so. Was I good looking? No, and hilariously so. Who the hell was this person behind me? They must be the biggest loser on earth! It was someone everyone in the class knew, that is, a big fat, athletically challenged, unattractive, feminine loser; I had no bloody idea. So I raced through twenty questions, all getting 'no's, and then looked around to see just who this fucking loser was.

'DAVID TIECK' was of course what was written on the board.

An hour out of my shell had been destroyed by my whole class, including my laughing-along teacher, who had just used theater sports to pick me apart and leave me with zero doubt that I was a piece of crap.

Fifteen years later, I took another improv class to prepare for interviews for my first book. It was utter love at second sight. Within two months I'd moved to New York to pursue it with my full heart. It was horrifically hard and yet I loved it. Truth be told, and even I am only realizing this as I write this, but my utter love of improv is something even more extreme—I can stand on a stage and make people laugh with words I am only thinking in this moment. To most people, attaining the ability to improvise scenes that make people laugh is like telling a quadriplegic he'll one day walk. To me, a seemingly incurable social phobic, it was like telling the quadriplegic he'll one day win the Olympic gold medal and world record for the hundred-meter sprint. And unfortunately over the past year, due to numerous circumstances, I've felt my improv comedy mojo disappear. I stopped working the muscle, and it got so weak I struggled to remember it existed. I needed to find it.

If you're a Muslim and you need spiritual guidance, you go to Mecca. If you're a sports lover and you need to be reminded of the joy of elite emotionally intense competition of the fittest, you go to the Superbowl or FA Cup final. If you need to make people laugh with things you make up in the moment, you need to go to the epicenter of the earthquake that created people like Tina Fey, Bill Murray, John Belushi, Chris Farley, Mike Meyers, Amy Pohler, Andy

Richter, Neil Flynn, Adam McCay and many, many more awesomely talented people, and that's in Chicago.

Only a few days earlier I had signed up for a five-day intensive at the famed and awesome iO Chicago, and when I walked into the theatre center, I was notably nervous. We were separated into our classes and began by going around the circle and explaining who we were and why we were there. Truth is I was so nervous about what I was going to say I barely listened to everyone else. Yet when it came to me I told a little bit about how I was so not supposed to be in the United States right now, and feared they may kick me out at any moment, and I got laughs, and they were heaven.

We got on stage and played some warm-up games, and I could feel the fun come back with every moment. Then we were told to do some brief fifteen-second scenes. I believe in the second or third I was involved with my scene partner and I were given the suggestion to play off of 'paper' so my scene partner mimed eating a piece of paper, and I joyfully announced, 'That's it, that's the entire bible!' Laughter rained upon us, we high-fived—scene over.

I was back, motherfucker! For the next five days I had the best of times and the most magnificent of times. I got to act out having an orgasm from having nail polish rubbed in my belly, I played a bad darts player on the way to a tournament obsessed with getting a bull's-eye first, I played a suicidal small kid planning his own funeral, I played part of a giant eye, and in the end I played a naive leprechaun in front of a packed audience and I was getting laughs from the exact same stage that a whole smorgasbord of my favorite comedians had started on.

Plus, I made some new amazing friends and laughed tons. Oh my God, I love it, my God I've missed it, and I simply have to find a way to make improvised comedy a significant part of my life. Plus, no one once made fun of me for not being an athlete. How could they? For one, I have won lots of sporting trophies since then, and two, in improv if you say you're the best athlete in the world then you ARE the best athlete in the world! And if you call your former classmates assholes everyone agrees with you! What a great thing it is.

YOU LEFT A PATCH

For all the sexual deviancy, obsessiveness and delinquency I have talked about in the previous pages, truth be told I am nothing less than a hopeless romantic. For as long as I can remember, there is nothing that has filled me with more joy than to lie in bed, cuddle up with a pillow, and imagine it is a girl whom I love and who loves me back, while we partake in a conversation based on the game 'I can be sweeter than you can be'. I've probably played this game ten thousand times now.

Hopeless romanticism is not healthy. It makes reality flawed. No one could ever possibly live up to the girl I see in the stains on the pillow. Yet any girl I ever meet and am attracted to, or especially the ones I lavid, and oh my God I lavided hard core the other night with the hostess at the Gotham Comedy Club in New York, and never saw her again, damnit (thank God my hotel has given me ample, soft supple pillows), well, they get over romanticized in my mind and then everything else falls short.

It's not just girls, either. I love to travel; clearly, it has been one of the joys of my life. This past couple of weeks, completely unwittingly, consciously at least, I have found myself on a bit of a tour of places I'd really love to live at some point of my life. I am now writing having just been in New York, a city I have 'known' I am destined to live in for a long, long time. It truly is the greatest city in the world, although, this time I failed to see the New York I have always romanticized in my mind.

It has occurred to me that all these bloody places I keep fantasizing about living in are usually because of certain small factors I love; improv in Chicago, the beauty of Vancouver, the history of Paris, the arts of New York, the bacon donuts of Portland— they're all awesome things, added to the wonder I feel whenever walking around strange streets, and meeting new people, or just being anonymous and I realize that once you get down to the real nitty gritty, day-to-day life in all these places would come down to work, familiar friends, and entertainment.

I have been down on my hometown for a few years now. It has some deep flaws, but everywhere does. Having spent my whole life in Sydney, I have been concentrating on the flaws, whereas in other cities I have been concentrating on the romantic notion of what they could be, where, truth be told, Sydney is simply one of the best places on earth, and all these other places have just as many, if not more, flaws.

I came to New York with a plan to perform stand-up a bunch of times. I thought it would be a nice bookend to the first chapter of this book, to see where I am now. I had this idea in my head that this would be easy; I could perform every night in awesome comedy clubs, full of great funny people, and still have time to see shows, and enjoy the city. But it's all crap. I just wrote a big long list of excuses why I didn't do it, but the reality is I chickened out.

I headed up to Toronto to see some friends I had met in Chicago and there I made even more awesome new friends, and had a lot of fun hanging around the Toronto improv scene. Then I jumped on a five day long train ride headed for Vancouver and watched snow and ice-covered lakes and wilderness race past my window, then flew to LA, then home.

I opened this book with a story of my first time performing stand-up and I'll finish it with my one timing performing stand-up in Australia. It did not go well. I had been performing stand-up a couple of times a week in LA, plus regular sketch and improv and so I had my chops working. But back in Australia I signed up then had a month to wait, a month where I foolishly did not perform anything, anywhere.

As the month went on, two things happened: I lost my stage legs, and I built this one performance up in my mind as make or break. Over the weeks I revised my act over and over and over, I had only five minutes so punch lines had to come fast, and they had to be huge.

As I walked onto the stage, first of the night after the host, a really tough spot, I found myself as nervous as I had ever been. My knees were shaking and my mind was racing, and I was not ready to have fun, the single most important factor when performing comedy.

I nervously started my first bit.

'I have just spent the past year living in LA, and when I told people I wanted to live there they would say to me, "I'd kill myself before I'd live in LA" and it occurred to me people say things like that all the time, I'd kill myself before I'd go to a Madonna concert, I'd kill myself before I'd wear pink pants," but if this is true, how come suicide notes aren't more fun?' (Always open with suicide). 'How come no woman has ever come home to find her husband dead on the floor next to a gun, brains splattered all over the walls, with a note that says "I TOLD YOU I'D KILL MYSELF BEFORE I WOULD EAT LOW FAT CHEESE AND I LOOK IN THE FRIDGE AND WHAT IS THERE – LIGHT CHEDDAR." Bang, splatter, dead.'

I got some laughs. *Some* laughs. This was one of my favorite bits, but I had only ever told it to other comedians, who are by nature darker and more ready to push boundaries far more than people in their thirties eating dinner on a Thursday at 7:30pm.

It was only now that it occurred to me that my act, as I had revised it and revised it over the past month, had gotten darker and dirtier every day. As I moved on, I talked about sex, and diseases, and things like, 'if you stick a can of coke up your ass and pull out a can of Pepsi you'll never lose a bet again in your life'. I knew it was the wrong crowd but I couldn't think of anything else. I was shaking, my voice was weak, and at one point a guy in the front row said to his friend, 'He's about to totally lose it.'

This prompted me to say the worst thing I have ever said on a stage. I had written a bunch of words on my hand to remind me of bits, and knowing how pathetic that looked, I had written a 'joke' about it as a saver, and as my set continued with its smattering of laughs from the more deviant people in the audience but groans or even worse silence from the rest, I said this: 'Oh, I have a bunch of things written on my hand, but don't worry it has nothing to do with my set, I was just planning on masturbating later and I find that if I pretend I am cheating on a school English exam it makes me less guilty thinking about twelve year old boys.' HUGE groans around the room! Instead of going with that and taking their side, 'Yes, you're all correct, that was a test of your morals and you all passed, except that guy over there in the red shirt, he giggled with glee. Got a secret to share with us all?' instead I said, 'I love groans,' then told a joke about chewing on Band-Aids, and compared scabs to the sweet chili sauce I could see on several people's plates, and jumped off stage.

It was a terrible, awful set, told to my biggest audience to date, and my first ever paying audience, and is and was the last time I ever performed anything in Australia. Plus, also just about the first time.

When I first conceived this project in January 2010 things were going really great for me. I was living in Los Angeles, chasing my dreams, confident and happy, enjoying my first ever long term relationship with a gorgeous girlfriend, I was spending most of my time around laughter, plentiful amounts of it being provoked by things I was saying, and I was feeling healthy and happy like I had never been before. As I end this project none of these things are true anymore. Whoops.

I've long been a fan of books about adventures of self growth and discovery - but I always wondered what would happen if someone went on a journey like this only for it all to go really bad. The weird thing was I didn't realize I was writing a story like this until reading it back later when I began to grasp just how dark and angry I had become. The journey started innocently enough, glamorous even. This despite going through an awful break up just before I began. Not good timing. And then, whether by coincidence and/ or as a consequence of my new obsession with trying to scrounge out and meticulously study every humiliating memory I had, or worse had till now blocked out, things began spiraling out of control, adventures gave way to desperate attempts to boast, laughter turned to tears, self loathing sessions elongated, love died, dreams died, friends, opportunities and my passions were lost, and bridges were burned, all while I got angrier, more bitter and grew chips on my shoulders like Australian tanning enthusiasts grow skin cancers.

I thought over and over about rewriting or repackaging these stories in ways to make me look better, or smarter, or saner and perhaps make them a touch more mass media marketable (my personal favorite incarnation was based on the most common theme of the year, and my life, titled *Something is Wrong with my Penis: True Stories of Mutual Hate*. Note: publishers had a different thought than 'favorite') – but truth is – screw that! That would be a lie. Instead if you made it this far, then you read my tale in its raw, largely unedited, still ful of grammer and spelling mistakes, and ultimately most truthful, angry and penis influenced form. I hope I made the right decision? Well probably not. Perhaps good decisions are not my forte? Still, I decided this counts as an attempt at some sort of a punk rock style rebellion, and it's probably more sanitary than my original idea to clean up the text but then wipe blood from a picked pimple on every copy.

I often don't know what the hell I am supposed to do in life, clearly, but I know these things:

- My optimism is coming back
- My bitterness and misplaced resentment is waning
- AIDs and cancer probably aren't actually funny
- Camels make really awful pets and
- I have unfinished business in Australia.

I still want to travel as much as possible. I still want to live and work around the world. My romantic notion of moving to a strange city to make it is over (for now, unless I win the US Greencard lottery, in which case—US, here I come!) but it's time to go home, get to work and show my own people what I have got, to figure out how to get paid to make people laugh (please, please don't make me have to get a real job again) and look forward to embarrassing myself, inevitably, many, many more times. You'll be the first to hear about it. Plus, in Sydney I have my own bed, and on my bed I have lots of really cuddly pillows.

Thanks for listening, everyone. I won't tell you to now go out and kill your own embarrassing memories, you scallywags, because it turns out that is very stupid thing to do, but I can leave you with one piece of advice that I *know* to be as wise as it is undeniably true: if you stick a pillow up your ass and when you pull it out you have a ukulele, then you have a serious problem and you should see a doctor immediately.

THE END

THE BOOK IS OVER, WHICH MEANS I'M CURED, RIGHT?

KNOCK; KNOCK

'What's that?'

'Wait, wait, Dave, it's one of your memories, a bad one, and you haven't murdered me yet—LET ME IN.'

'Who is it? Who is out there?'

'It's your penis!'

'Oh, I have already spoken far too much about you! Go away.'

'But no, you forgot something, I'm not *actually* your penis, just a memory of it, it's important!'

'Oh forget it, the book is done, if it was that big a deal it would have come up at some point of the year. I'm closing this now, go away.'

'YOU USED TO PISS ON THE WALL!'

'Wait, what are you talking about? The time I was so busting for a piss and the Burger King wouldn't let me use the bathroom unless I bought something first, and promising to buy something later wouldn't appease them, and actually buying something first would have definitely resulted in pissing my pants at the counter, so instead I snuck into a storeroom/janitor's closet and pissed on the wall?'

'No, no, no, and even I, a story about your penis, isn't completely sure you should tell people you did that.'

243

'Well, I'm not *proud* of it, am I? I was busting, and a little pissed off. I am one of the biggest consumers of fast food in the world, and I have never once used one of their bathrooms without a purchase. I never even leave my tray for them to put in the trash. A little respect was all I wanted!'

'Yes, yes, piss in their closet, great way to *earn* respect.'

'Ok, thank you, I'm going now, and you, stupid little penis story, can fuck off.'

'YOU WERE CIRCUMCISED TWICE!'

'What?'

'Well, actually, I don't know the full story, because they cut my head off! Get it? Little circumcision joke there.'

'Ha ha, that's actually kind of genius! But are you talking about the time when I was three or four years old?'

'Yes, and there was something wrong with your penis, something about the head, and you could not urinate straight to save your life. It didn't matter where you pointed it, it could go in any direction at all and there was no way to control it.'

'That's right…. I remember being really ashamed of it, even at that age, and knowing my family were trying to NOT get mad at me, but were clearly worried, although I don't know if you can actually think that clearly at that age. So, what happened?'

'Don't you remember, being probably four years old, so already old enough to have full conversations, and have fully formed memories, when you were sitting on the stairs crying your little eyes out, your penis hurting so much, because your penis had been so weird that they had to operate on it? You were compensated by being allowed to eat whatever you wanted and that this was great but probably not worth it.'

'I remember. What the hell did the doctors do? Did they just open up the hole wider? Had I not been circumcised and now I was? Was I actually circumcised for a second time? Was it like a two-blade razor, the first blade lifts up the foreskin and trims it but it's the second blade, when you're old enough to really have your psyche affected by the knowledge you're about to have a piece of your penis cut off, that really results in a close shave? Does Gillette owe my penis a billion dollars?'

'How the hell do I know? I'm just a horrible memory.'

'If you don't know, then why are you here?'

'I want you to murder me, please. I've spent thirty years jumping all over your sub-conscious making sure you'll never have a good relationship with your actual penis or anything that goes near it, while simultaneously reminding you that one way to reduce physical and mental pain is to eat a lot of bad-for-you food, even though it never works!'

'You're right! This whole shambles may have been YOUR fault to begin with. Come here, you little shit, I'm going to fucking KILL YOU!!!!!!!'

'Yes, yes, that's the spirit—shoot me, stab me, and make it messy and quick!'

'Where's my gun? Oh, wait, it's a memory. All right, I'm imagining a gun right now, and you better believe it's a big motherfucker!'

'YES, YES, put it up against my head, blow my brains out, make ME DEAD, NOW, NOW, NOW!!'

'BOOM, BOOM, BOOM! Splash. Mess. Corpse!'

NOW we're done!

(PS—Don't worry, I know a little something about guns. When I was a teenager I spent a couple of months in my upper middle-class-sponsored teens secretly hoping to become a gangster rapper. I'd tell you more but there are some things even *I'm* too embarrassed to talk about.)